The Headteacher from Hell and Other Animals

David E. Hellawell

PUBLISHING The Questions Publishing Company Ltd,
C O M P A N Y Birmingham

©1996 The Questions Publishing Company Limited
27 Frederick Street, Birmingham B1 3HH

ISBN 1-898149-62-3

Designed and typeset by
The Questions Publishing Company Ltd.
Illustrations by Iqbal Aslam
Printed at Questions Publishing

About the author

This is the second collection of the sometimes humorous writings on school management of David Hellawell. This is, of course, only the pseudonym of an internationally celebrated bon vivant whose real name is the toast of café society in most of the capital cities in continental Europe. He claims that he writes these pieces as a form of penance for the life he used to lead before his stupendous win in the UK National Lottery freed him to pursue his present career as boulevardier or man about town. His fatal attractiveness as far as the opposite sex is concerned is the stuff of legend in the coffee houses of Prague, Budapest, and Sofia; and if you can believe this, or anything else beyond the first sentence of this blurb (which is also dubious), you fully deserve to be paying him the royalties which he is staking out weekly on the off-chance that these dreams might become reality after all.

Dedication

To my sons Nicholas and Martin without whose constant encouragement and constructive criticism I might have been writing books like this in the 1960s rather than the 1990s.

Acknowledgements

I would like to thank Liz John and Caroline Williams, past and present editors of *Managing Schools Today*, and Howard Sharron of Questions Publishing for their continuing support. My thanks are again also due to Iqbal Aslam for the excellent cartoons.

Contents

Preface

THE OVERWHELMING majority of the articles collected in this book were first published in *Managing Schools Today* magazine and its predecessor *School Governor* between 1990 and 1996. Not least among the many changes in education during this period has been the name given to the responsible Ministry. The author and editors believe that to leave DES, DfE, DfEE and other titles, initials and acronyms as they were when the articles were written will convey something of the changing nature of the times.

In the years leading up to 1989, there were rich varieties of jokes circulating in the then Communist-controlled countries of Central and Eastern Europe which were usually classified under the generic label of 'black humour'. In the main, the witticisms were protests against the particular leader or leading politicians of the country concerned. So there were many quips current in what was then the German Democratic Republic against Erich Honecker, the so-called General Secretary, and also against his wife, who was, for a time, the least well qualified Minister of Education in a nation where education and qualifications had both been taken very seriously for at least the past two centuries. When a large hole was dug in front of the Ministry of Education in

Berlin, it was alleged that the workmen were searching for Mrs Honecker's missing degrees and diplomas.

Sometimes the jokes were directed against Communist countries in an even more parlous economic state than the joke teller's and, for most of the 70s and 80s, it was a fair bet that Romania was the bottom of the dung heap. Hence the question as to what the Romanians used for lighting before they had candles. The answer to this was, of course, electricity. There were also the jibes universally current in the then USSR and its satellite states along the lines of: 'You pretend to pay us, and we pretend to work'.

As this last dictum sums up quite precisely one of the main reasons why these Communist regimes eventually collapsed so dramatically, it is evident that there was a very serious undercurrent to what an older tradition more aptly called 'gallows humour'. Jokes of this kind were often one of the only few possible forms of protest against the political system when the mass media were closed to any kind of criticism of the authorities. I used to attempt to enliven what was no doubt a dull lecture on the state of *Mitteleuropa* under Communism by quoting quips which encapsulated, with the brevity of wit, the message I was trying to put across at what probably seemed interminable length. I find the term 'gallows humour' so apt because it conveys the message that those under sentence of death can often see a funny side to what seems like a very grim situation indeed to the objective onlooker.

Breeding ground

I like to think that my own comic pieces in this and my earlier collection *Total School Mis-management* are firmly in the gallows humour tradition. Certainly I think that the state of education in England and Wales over the last twenty years at least has been a rich breeding ground for such humour. I remember going into a school the day after it had been announced that Kenneth Clarke was to be reshuffled from Health to Education as part of his glorious ministerial career. The white board in the staff room contained the following graffiti:

Question: what do you call a man who won't listen to his

doctors? Answer: the Secretary of State. Didn't we do well?

It has, after all, been almost as easy in Margaret Thatcher's and John Major's England as it was in Erich Honecker's GDR to make very dark 'jokes' about the state of education, and the teachers under these regimes have been very quick to do so. This is very largely because, more than at any other time in recent English history, there has been an 'official government line' on education which has not only been put into practice in a much more relentless fashion than heretofore, but has been predominant across large parts of the mass media. In response, there have been, circulating around staff rooms up and down the country, 'samizdat' hand-outs of fiendish ingenuity which have sometimes very wittily mocked the more obvious stupidities of, for example, a centrally imposed National Curriculum in England and Wales. The careful reader will have observed that I am consistently excluding Scotland and Northern Ireland, because like L. P. Hartley's past, these are other countries, at least as far as education is concerned, and they do things differently there.

If you pretend to consult the populace and then totally ignore its voice, as was the case with the initial National Curriculum 'consultation exercise', you must expect that the victims will make their voices heard in other ways. There must have been times during the early years of the National Curriculum when successive Education Ministers in London would have longed for the prospect of Bertolt Brecht's proposed 'solution' to the Communist authorities of the GDR when the *Volk* was at its most disaffected; namely to dissolve the electorate and start again with a new one. (Actually, there were times when the dissolution of the existing teaching force did indeed appear to be the favoured strategy of the Conservative powers that be. Certainly the dissolution of the LEAs, starting with ILEA, has seemed firmly on the cards throughout these years.)

The more the authorities put out sanitised versions of what is really going on, the more the inmates will be spurred on to produce the unauthorised versions. These serve not only as a means of telling those outside not to believe the official lies, but also as a source of therapy for those inside who are compelled to live the official lie in public. The gap between the rhetoric and the reality is the fertile dark swamp from which the jokes emerge into the daylight.

This is as true of authoritarian institutions as it is of totalitarian states. (Many of the wittiest of the dissidents have found the source of their humour drying up very rapidly since the collapse of the old Stalinist regimes in Europe. Some of them would no doubt welcome back the official censors as the necessary flint on which to spark off the witticisms. Perhaps this is one of the reasons why the apparently reconstructed ex-Communists are making something of a comeback in many of these states?) There is what Gerard Egan has called a 'shadow side' to organisations, where team building becomes the management of cliques and information sharing becomes gossip, rumour and the grapevine. The more the official line bears resemblance to the worst estate agent rhetoric about the des. res., the more prevalent and the wider in scope will be the shadow side. Much of this collection is about this shadow side to the management of schools which have more than their fair share of official organisational rhetoric.

A lot of this rhetoric flows from the headteachers of the land, who will sometimes outdo their political masters in trying to put a gloss on the often grimy reality. This tendency has become ever more pronounced since government policy has been hell-bent on subjecting education to what are risibly called 'market forces'. Lying has been sanctioned as 'public relations', and many heads can now justify the 'window dressing' of their schools, at least to themselves, as part of their duty to preserve the jobs of their staffs.

The burden of responsibility

The headteacher from hell is no doubt as far removed from the norm as is the secular saint which he or she is made out to be on the rare occasions when the tabloid press wakes up to the enormous responsibilities which modern society places on his or her shoulders. Nevertheless, the very possibility of the headteacher from hell is just one more demonstration of life's little ironies to which this collection is really dedicated.

To return to my earlier *Mitteleuropa* theme, and to illustrate my penchant for writing implausibly long sentences, I recall that, as a fashionably moody teenager, I became fascinated by a writer who appeared to depict life's angst like nobody else. When you settle in the early 1950s on a Czech writer from Prague who wrote in German; who rarely finished anything longer than a short story; who wanted what he had written to be burned when he died in 1924; who had the good sense to be born Jewish when the coming regime in Germany, not to mention the *Reichsprotectorate* of Bohemia and Moravia, was not into buying or promoting books written by Jews (it was actually into burning the books first and their authors thereafter); and who also had the good sense to be anti-totalitarian when the coming regime after the coming regime's literary censorship was going to make Hitler's Germany seem positively libertarian by comparison; when this is the schlemiel you eventually choose to write about for your Master's thesis in your early twenties, you do not expect him in your own lifetime to become the centre of a tourist trade, complete with Franz Kafka T-shirts and Franz Kafka biscuit tins, etc.

Yet I did, indeed, see this development occur in the years between 1990 and 1992 on the streets of Prague, as market forces began to transform the non-commercialism of that splendid city. From being almost a non-person in his home town, Kafka became the centre of a flourishing business which began to emulate the Shakespeare industry in Stratford upon Avon.

Biscuit tins notwithstanding, I have long maintained that Kafka's unfinished novels *The Trial* and *The Castle* are much better management primers than any of the current texts by the management gurus of our time. To paraphrase: 'Somebody must have been spreading lies about headteacher K because one morning, without having done anything wrong, he was informed by OFSTED inspectors that his school was failing.' The subsequent attempts to find meaning in an apparently meaningless world, where absurd bureaucracies come to incomprehensible decisions which the headteacher then has to manage, are what this collection is really all about. Some have argued that we are all now living in the nightmare world which Kafka described. I am not so optimistic.

The intelligent governor's guide to educational acronyms

ONE OF THE many problems for a new school governor trying to come to grips with the world of education is that its jungle of acronyms is well nigh impenetrable. No official statement seems complete without a liberal scattering of NCCs, TVEIs, SATs, LMSs and the like. Indeed, one school governor of my acquaintance was so frustrated in her early days in her new role by the plethora of acronyms with which she was confronted in her reading that she began to refer to them as agronyms.

What should the new governor do to cope with this problem? The first lesson to grasp is that there is no need to be daunted by the prospect of having to learn what all these acronyms mean. Keep insisting on the full versions being used in meetings. These full versions are themselves not exactly instantly meaningful. The acronyms were not, in any case, invented to improve the means of communication in education. Their originators had a different purpose in mind. Never forget George Bernard Shaw's dictum that all professions are a conspiracy against the layman. Why did doctors write their prescriptions in illegibly scrawled dead languages? Why do lawyers use arcane terms like 'torts'? You can safely bet that it is not an attempt to create a world in which man shall speak plainly unto man (or perhaps person to person in these politically correct times?), but rather to create a mystique and to keep the layperson at bay (at the latter's expense, of course).

The educational professional has had a hard time of it in this respect. Ever since the days when the teacher was a cleric doing a bit of moonlighting, and the textbook could still be a chained bible from which suitable verses could be read out in Latin, it's been downhill all the way into intelligibility. In recent times it had got to the point where some parent governors actually began to believe that they knew what was going on in the classroom. Indeed it is darkly rumoured in some quarters that there are a few schools where the sign: 'No Parents Beyond This Point' has been removed, and some parents are actually to be seen in the classroom itself.

Now somebody had to put a stop to this dangerous nonsense, and there is clear evidence that the counter-reformation began at the top. Informed sources assure me that some anonymous London mandarin confided in his cups to the barmaid at the Rose and Crown that he was worried that the DES was going to be taken over by the DTI because education was now viewed by his political masters as a sub-standard widget-producing process that they could clearly see was in need of drastic restructuring if it were not to end in bankruptcy. The barmaid's perplexed and perplexing response to this was to enquire, with a touch of that grace and charm for which she was famous in the locality, what the hell he was talking about. She didn't know what the DES was when it was at home, but she assured him that she was an expert on the DTs and there were few signs as yet that his condition was as terminal in that respect as he appeared to fear.

It was then that the aforesaid mandarin had his flash of inspiration. If a whole new set of acronyms were invented that no-one could understand, then the Department of Education and Science would have a secure future as the only authorised interpreters of the truth as revealed to the faithful in Elizabeth House. Thus it came to pass that the fastest growing section in the house that Poulson built became no longer 'Schools 3' but 'Acronyms 4'. A whole team of civil servants now labours night and day to produce not only acronyms, but acronyms of acronyms (this was the deadly mark two version of the acronym, as in TRIST, which was supposed to mean TVEI-related INSET (!?), and which flew faster than the speed of sound and appeared in print before anyone had time to construct any form of Star Wars defence system).

These creative souls are justly proud of the recent Queen's Award for Industry bestowed upon them as the Ministry of Disinformation. The essential trick of their trade is to have one set of official meanings for the acronyms which appear unintelligible to the lay public, while having a totally different set of very clear meanings known only to the initiated in the sacred temple.

I have, however, after seconds of back-breaking toil, been able to crack the incredibly complex 'enigma' code and I am now able to reveal the 'real' versions which lie behind the official acronyms. Here are just a few examples:

	Official Version	**Real Meaning**
LMS	Local Management of Schools	Hell of a Mess
LFM	Local Financial Management	Hell of a Fine Mess
SAT	Standard Assessment Task	Stupefyingly Arduous Testing
SEAC	School Examinations and Assessment Council	South East Asian Conundrums
SOA	Statement of Attainment	Son of A ...
TA	Teacher Assessment	Thanks for doing the work for no extra financial reward.
KS4	Key Stage Four	Unclimbed Himalayan peak.
AWPU	Age Weighted Pupil Units	Absent Without Public Understanding (i.e. still countable).
ERA	Education Reform Act	ERAdicate (e.g. learning, civilisation as we know it.)
NCC*	National Curriculum Council	Rock Group (As in (TE)N CC)
ASB	Aggregated Schools Budget	Amalgamated Savings Bank
GSB	General Schools Budget	God Save the Buildings
TGAT	Task Group on Assessment And Testing	Thank God And Thatcher

* N.B. There is some dispute about this one, as a few interpreters hold that NCC is DESspeak for Newcastle Cricket Club. This seems unlikely, however, as the average London civil servant's impression of climatic conditions in Tyne and Wear is such that organised cricket would be considered impossible in those latitudes.

It should be fully understood that these are only early prototypes and that we can expect more advanced models to be rolling off the DES production line in the months and years ahead. Watch this space!

The headteacher as absentee landlord

WHEN I FIRST began teaching, many moons ago, there was a lovely story current amongst the old lags on the teaching force at the time which ought to have been true, so I shall recount it as if it were gospel. It concerned a headteacher to whom we shall give the *nom de plume* of Fred to spare the blushes of any of his family still able to identify his activities after all this time. Similarly, I have used Wallsend, Bolton and Whitehaven as the venues for his story, although these were not, in reality, the exact locations of our tale.

I was reminded of the saga of 'Fred' when I noted that, amongst all those interviewed during the 50th anniversary Second World War victory celebrations on the loose theme of 'How I really enjoyed the war years', there was one elderly gentleman who bemoaned the outbreak of peace in 1945 on the grounds that it had removed many of the lovely opportunities for scams which the war years had provided. This feeling may not have been reserved for 'spivs' operating on the wartime black market.

There was at least one headteacher, namely our Fred, who may have regretted the cessation of hostilities in the same way that some of the underworld citizens of Chicago in the 1920s were long in mourning for the ending of the 'noble experiment', ie: the prohibition of the sale and manufacture of alcoholic beverages in the USA. He had been appointed to a headship of a Secondary school at Wallsend in the years immediately preceding the second World War. On returning triumphant from his interview to his home in Bolton, he was, however, astonished to discover that his wife did not share his sense of elation. She had apparently only consented to his going for interview because of her private conviction that he didn't stand a chance of being appointed. Now he had been successful, she had to break the news that there was no way she was going to depart for Geordieland under any circumstances whatsoever.

He was equally adamant that he was not going to pass up this promotion and all the increase in money that went with it. He was convinced that, if he stuck firmly to his guns, his good lady wife would ultimately have to give in and find a new nest in the wide open lands of Northumbria.

So it was that, some months later, he began what promised to be an endless period of time when he would have to commute weekly by rail between two towns on opposite sides of the UK and with more miles between them than could be easily covered by motor car, at a time long before motorways gave at least the illusion of geographical mobility and accessibility.

Battleaxe

This, by the way, gives the lie to the theory that, before feminism and assertiveness training for the female of the species, women dutifully obeyed their husband's every whim and command. Not in Lancashire they didn't. Les Dawson's jokes about his mother-in-law may not be accepted as scientific proof of the existence of the legendary species of the Lancashire battleaxe, but there is archival documentary evidence in the shape of countless picture postcards of the henpecked little husband and his formidable spouse. I recall these as being very popular in the Blackpool of my youth, when my parent's generation could find lots of echoes of many of the domestic situations which surrounded them. As

George Orwell pointed out, in his celebrated essay on these picture postcards entitled *The Art of Donald McGill:* 'Next to sex, the henpecked husband is the favourite joke.'

But I digress. To return to Fred sadly learning the error of his ways, life only became manageable by his catching a very early morning train indeed and arriving at school at about 10.30 on Monday mornings. Departure time from school at the end of each week was around 3.30 on Friday evenings. Four nights of the week he spent in lodgings in the North East. At least by these means, he could continue to maintain his residence in his home town and thereby preserve his marriage at a time when divorce was viewed in most quarters as incompatible with the state of headship. He appeared to be doomed to this existence up to retirement, because those were the days when leaving one secondary headship for another within a decade was also about as unthinkable as serial monogamy.

Then came the outbreak of Hitler's war, and when the Luftwaffe began its policy of *Bomben über England,* Tyneside caught a fairly early packet of what unfortunately seemed like the shape of things to come. If Londoners could evacuate their offspring to far-flung corners of the English and Welsh countryside, then Tynesiders could certainly evacuate children across to Whitehaven, which did not appear to be on Adolf's hit list at the time. So, as a first stage process, the 'lower school' of Fred's educational emporium was shifted across that relatively narrow strip of land which separates the east and west coasts of England at that point (a convenient geographical feature noted some centuries before by a Roman by the name of Hadrian, which accounts for a town being called Wallsend).

Goering . . . Goering . . . gone

By the time this operation had been planned and carried out, however, it was noticeable that fires were no longer lighting the night sky along the Tyne. Feldmarschall Hermann Goering was finding his air force was in greater demand in other parts of the theatre of war by this time, and Tyneside was somewhat neglected by the German military high command as a bombing target from this point onwards. So the 'senior pupils' stayed in Wallsend, leaving the school on two sites for the duration of the hostilities. Even if Hadrian had worked out that his wall was going to be a shorter distance across the country in this neck of the woods than anywhere else, the 73 miles distance from Wallsend to the other end of the wall in the west still leaves your average split-site comprehensive looking a good deal more cosily together than Fred's far-flung empire was from 1942 to 1945.

So we now have Fred with a triangular geographical conundrum to solve. Some of the time, he was expected to be at the upper school in Wallsend, some of the time he had to keep an eye on what was happening at the lower school in Whitehaven, and at weekends he was in Bolton. Fred was not lacking in ingenuity in this situation. This was borne home on his staff not long before VE day, when one of the teachers working in Whitehaven was back on Tyneside for the weekend and happened to meet a colleague who had stayed in Wallsend when they bumped into each other in Northumberland Street in Newcastle-upon-Tyne. The first colleague commiserated with the second colleague about the fact that the latter and his mates had had to put up with having Fred around the place nearly all the time in recent years, while the good pedagogues in Whitehaven had been running what amounted to a self-governing breakaway state in the almost total absence of Fred during this period.

The second colleague then gently broke the news that the Wallsend brigade had harboured very similar feelings vis-a-vis their erstwhile colleagues in Whitehaven, where they had imagined Fred had been almost permanently ensconced looking after the welfare of the younger kiddy-winkies exiled to the south of the Solway Firth. The subsequent supposition on all sides was that Bolton had seen a great deal more of Fred during the war than had been the case in peacetime. So the fact that Fred's retirement was almost exactly simultaneous with Hitler's suicide in the Berlin bunker may not have been entirely coincidental.

Dr. Fear

As an afterthought, there should be some research done into the correlation between school effectiveness and the absence of headteachers. I have a sneaking suspicion that the correlation might not be negative in some cases. Certainly there are some heads on the national talk circuit who appear to operate as absentee landlords for significant periods of time but whose schools seem like models of learning organisations. Or maybe I've just listened too much to their media sound bites? Nevertheless, I do think there is something to be said for the 'Dr Fear' syndrome.

In my younger days, I had occasion to visit infrequently a school where the head allegedly gloried in what seemed then like the title of a James Bond thriller. It may have been coincidence, but 'Dr Fear' was never present in the school on the occasion of any of my visits. This may simply mean, of course, that his secretary was not going to have me wasting his valuable time by actually engaging him in what she presumed would be idle chitchat, but I did begin to wonder whether there were not more sinister games afoot. Perhaps the staff had done away with the previous incumbent and invented this new and most unlikely title-holder? Or perhaps it was a more mundane case of the LEA economising by putting a nameplate on a door instead of a real person behind it?

Whatever the motive, the effects were readily visible. The pupils slowed their pace to a decidedly cowed crawl when passing by the unhallowed portal. I should imagine that they responded very readily to any threat that they might be sent to Dr Fear. It must have seemed like a summons to enter the jaws of hell. Far better in these circumstances for Dr Fear not to appear in possibly quite nondescript person.

The fact that he was never actually seen during daylight hours could only add to the terror-stricken legends about this mysterious being. If he did actually exist, I think the staff should have clubbed together to pay him to stay off the premises. Certainly, the day he was seen by the pupils not to be one of the living dead must have been the day disciplinary standards took a nosedive in that school.

Referee I wuz robbed

IN MY EARLY years of teaching in schools, I fairly often heard older members of staff going through the 'poor teacher – good reference' routine. This was their standard way of explaining the alleged incompetence of some of those in high places in education. The argument, in short – and in those days it was usually in long – was that those teachers whom heads were desperate to get rid of were the fortunate recipients of excellent references to speed them on their way.

I interpreted this as the kind of mythology spread around by those who had failed to reach those high places themselves and who were in real need of some psychological balm to spread on their damaged sense of self-esteem. As far as I was concerned, the very idea was so far-fetched that it only served to expose their own inadequacies.

Later, I recall gaining an insight into perspectives on the opposite side of the same coin when I sat in a public meeting, where a headteacher spoke of the happy family atmosphere in her school. She claimed that this was self-evident from the length of time which most of 'my excellent staff' had been working at the school.

I happened to be sitting next to a teacher at this school at the time, and she immediately whispered in my ear with a remarkable degree of dulcet bitterness: 'That's only because she gives us all such lousy references.'

Now I'm in the ranks of the wrinklies myself, and, for good or for bad in the light of what follows, not dissatisfied with the way my own career has developed. But I'm not so sure now that the notion of good and bad references for the wrong reasons is all myth. Admittedly I have only a few clues to go on but, for all the obvious reasons, that's all that most of us ever accumulate about the darker corners of educational politics. So, for what they are worth, here are my scraps of what is, for the most part, hearsay evidence about the great reference mystery. The difference between most of the following anecdotes and the stories I heard in the staff rooms of my youth is that in these cases I now recount I know my sources very well, and I tend to believe what they say.

Item one is the existence in one case of two references held on file for the same member of staff. In the eyes of most, if not all, of her colleagues this good lady had drawn a weak hand when the cards of social and interpersonal skills were dealt out. Any group in which she operated had as little chance of becoming a functioning team as the former Yugoslav government. So why should there have been two different references on file for her? Well, one reference was for heads in the near vicinity, who were either likely to be on the local information grapevine about such characters or likely to be not averse to kicking up an embarrassing fuss were they to be landed with a parcel of trouble on the strength of a false bill of goods. The second reference was for all the other heads.

Item two was a reference drawn to the attention of someone I know very well some years after she had been working in the secondary school that had appointed her *in spite of* the most perfunctory of references from her previous head. The reference in question apparently read: 'Mrs. Z joined the staff of this school in 19.. and worked here for five years.' Nothing more.

Above and beyond

In this particular case, the teacher concerned had worked, to my certain knowledge, in an extremely diligent and capable fashion for these five years in her previous school. Indeed, to say that she had worked above and beyond the normal call of duty would be an understatement. She had also been praised publicly by this head on more than one occasion for her efforts, so there was no question of her contributions going unnoticed. She had, for example, successfully taken the first cohort of sixth form pupils in the school to 'A' level in her subject.

Yet any normal reading of the reference would have suggested that there was little if anything positive that could be said about her. It might even have indicated that there were actually a number of sinister aspects to her record that were best not put on paper. It was the extreme good fortune of this candidate that she was initially interviewed for what was, in any case, then only a temporary appointment *before* this particular reference arrived. At the interview, she was practically assured of the job pending the arrival of satisfactory references. She was, therefore, more than a little surprised to be called back for a second interview which turned out to be a further very serious grilling.

It was only much later, in what eventually turned into a very productive six years in the new school, that the solution to the mystery of why she had been called back for a second interview was revealed to her. Presumably, the panel that appointed her to this new job had other reference evidence to set against the reference in question, as well as the evidence of their own eyes and ears at the two interviews. Nevertheless, the suspicion remains that if references had been read before some of the applicants were called to interview, then this candidate might never have been interviewed in the first place. What is more, this could have been the end result of all the other applications she made for posts where she gave her previous head as a referee. It is worth underlining at this stage that she had not the slightest reason to suspect that she would be given anything other than a most satisfactory reference.

The motive behind this reference was not one of retention at all costs, because the teacher in question had already moved for domestic reasons to another part of the country when the reference was requested. Nor do I think it was a simple case of idleness or negligence or whatever it is that causes references not to be sent at all – a phenomenon I personally have encountered more than once in a long career of taking up references, and once is more than enough for comfort in this respect in my view. In this particular instance, other hearsay evidence followed up later suggests that this head held bizarre views about any teachers who were clearly improving standards in *his* school, but who then actually dared to leave what he regarded as his personal fiefdom. They were regarded by him as individuals who were guilty of committing an act of such base treachery that from then on they were *persona non grata* as far as he was concerned. Most of the time, this particular brand of paranoia was reasonably well hidden.

Chasm

Item three concerns a teacher who was appointed to a post largely on the personal recommendation of a member of staff who had worked with her in her previous school. After being told she had

13

got the job, she was taken to one side by one of the deputies, the friend of the friend, who declared himself offended on her account by the gap, not to say yawning chasm, between the written reference they had received from her head and not only the personal recommendation but also her performance at interview. In high dudgeon, she returned to her school and asked to see a copy of the reference which the head had sent, only to be met by his response that this was not possible because he had conveyed only an oral reference over the phone. She had half expected to be rebuffed, but to be confronted with what she knew to be a barefaced lie quite took her breath away. The incident certainly lent credence to the widely held view within that school that the head was not only in the habit of not giving good references to the staff he wanted to keep, but that some of the thorns in his flesh had moved onward and upward surprisingly quickly.

Finally, item four. A former close colleague of mine was once personally told by the head of his outfit, whom we will call Bill, that someone in his department, whom we will call Fred, had applied for a job elsewhere, and he would be sure to give him a good reference, wouldn't he? This was said, as it was reported to me, with considerable intensity of feeling and absolutely no irony. As my friend personally held Fred in very high regard, there was no conflict or dilemma for him in this request; indeed, quite the reverse.

However, he was only too well aware that for some time Bill and Fred had hardly been on speaking terms. Fred had made it publicly clear in no uncertain terms that he deplored the managerial conduct of Bill on a particularly contentious issue, and he had been making life very difficult for the latter ever since. The seething resentment of Bill in return was made no less clear, but in his case privately. (In retrospect, my colleague can't make up his mind to this day whether, on this particular managerial issue, Bill was highly courageous, downright foolhardy or deviously clever to the nth degree!) In my colleague's view it was one of those most difficult of managerial confrontations, when there was right, as well as wrong, on both sides.

There was no doubt in my colleague's mind, however, that Bill wanted to get rid of Fred at all costs, and that the request for him to do a favourable reference was not at all a sign of the magnanimity of a benevolent autocrat. He was being given the modern equivalent of a 'will no one rid me of this turbulent priest?' outburst. In a modern world, in which you are not allowed to give individuals the key to the gun cupboard or to send them a silken cord on a cushion, and where hari kari or self-immolation on your manager's behalf are distinctly out of fashion, the glowing reference may be the only sure fire exit message. It is a fair assumption that Bill and my colleague were the two referees for Fred (you had to list the head of your outfit as one of the referees in this particular case, which is doubtless why Bill knew of the application in the first place) – in which case, I have a firm belief that Fred had two splendid references to help him on his way to what was a very considerable, and no doubt well deserved, promotion. I am equally certain that only one of those references was totally sincere.

The moral of this cautionary tale would appear to be that all references should carry the equivalent of a Government Health Warning.

Right face, right place

THERE IS A rumour going around to the effect that once all the schools in the land have been privatised, they will be declared exempt from any of those tedious and tiresome equal opportunities laws. This will save governing bodies a lot of bother. You will, in future, be able to advertise yourself as 'An Unequal Opportunities Employer' and there will be an 'Unequal Opportunities Agency' whose aim it will be to provide you with help and guidance in this respect.

I have been privileged to have a glimpse at a draft of the handbook on *How To Make Unequal Appointments*, which is due to be issued at some point in the future when the government's reform programme has been completed. Here are a few extracts:

The application form

This should be sent out only to applicants who enclose a stamped, addressed envelope. Why should you put the school to any unnecessary expense? In any case, you are likely to be flooded by applicants in these times of suitably high unemployment. Never forget that you are in a buyer's market and it's the applicants who are desperate to sell themselves as the ideal occupant of the post you are offering.

The application form must be designed so that you can screen out the unsuitable as quickly as possible. Asking all applicants to enclose a recent colour photograph of themselves will save you a lot of boring reading (and possible later embarrassment), but the following headings are also useful for the reasons given.

Name: You might be surprised to discover how many candidates can be ruled out at this first obstacle by following a few of our simple precepts. Quite apart from the obvious unsuitability of anyone called Wayne or Kylie, the name of the applicant alone can often provide you with enough clues to save you the trouble of reading through the answers to later questions. We are reliably informed that in Belfast, the name alone is enough to also tell you immediately all you need to know about the applicant's likely address, religion and political affiliation. It's such a pity that this efficient coding system isn't universal as yet.

Address: We all know where in our own areas are the kinds of homes which are likely to produce people of decent breeding. You will be delighted to learn that our *Estate Agent's Guide To Desirable Residences* does this same job on a nationwide basis.

Date of Birth: The last thing you want to do is to employ a set of wrinklies. Your establishment is not a rest home on the Costa Geriatrica. You only want to employ those who can't remember the days when employees actually had rights and not just obligations. The beauty about the newer generations is that they don't know any better.

Marital Status: If you're careful, you can learn a lot about the sloppy personal lives of your applicants. It's useful to provide boxes to be ticked so they know just what you're asking, for example:

Married ☐
Never married ☐
Separated ☐
Divorced ☐
Spouse deceased ☐
Cohabiting ☐
Remarried ☐
Into adultery and/or serial monogamy in a big way ☐
Bigamous ☐
Polygamous ☐

(Allow ticks in more than one box and between boxes if in intermediate status.)

Religion: Do not provide boxes here because there are just too many weirdo sects to cover. Any answer which suggests the applicant will not be a willing, not to say zealous (but not too zealous), participant in the daily act of worship means the applicant is out. This act of worship is going to reflect the predominantly Christian nature of the Secretary of State's concept of the religious condition of the nation, so you will need to have handy our *Guide to Acceptable and Accredited forms of Christianity.*

Dependents: A trick question designed to trap the unwary into a response. Any answer other than 'none and none on the way' is a wrong answer. Children and other relatives can be such a distraction from work, especially for mothers. Single mothers, of course, are by definition unfit to be allowed to teach children.

Hobbies: You can do a very useful winnowing job here. Such activities as whippet racing are clearly only engaged in by untouchables, but an entry such as 'the sport of kings' might require more careful follow-up.

The answer you are really looking for will be along the lines of 'my work is my hobby', but you will have to do some careful cross-checking to ensure that this kind of response is not fraudulent. It is normally possible, for example, to take such an answer at its face value if it is written by a nun in holy orders. Nuns have been found to make excellent employees, by the way, as they are usually prepared to work from dawn to dusk for very little financial recompense, and you are unlikely to have to worry about the fortnight's maternity leave still allowed by our somewhat antiquated laws. (The Parliamentary bill to compel women to relinquish their occupations after childbirth is still only wending its way slowly through its first reading in the House of Commons at the time of writing.)

Educational Experience: The one thing to watch out for here is any indication that the applicants have actually been through a course of teacher training at anything remotely resembling an institution of higher education (HE). This would clearly render them unfit for work in your establishment. It was precisely to stamp out this form of infection (MTD or Mad Teacher Disease) that the government finally severed completely the links between HE and teacher training. Go for one of the new indentured apprentices instead; preferably one you have trained in your own school. Ex-pupils of your own scholastic emporium are ideal for these purposes, as they are unlikely to have been contaminated by exposure to other educational influences.

Previous Employment: 'None' is the best answer of all here. Not only are new entrants to the 'profession' much more malleable, they also come even cheaper than the average pedagogue. If such candidates are unfortunately unavailable, then at all costs avoid those applicants who have worked in the state sector under the old LEA system. They are bound to have picked up a range of bad habits which it will be the very devil to root out.

References: Under no circumstances should you allow applicants to indicate that they do not wish their present employer to be approached for a reference. That only increases everybody's phone bills. Make it obligatory.

Additional information and personal statement: Insist that this is handwritten and not photocopied, to ensure that the more idle brethren are compelled to put pen to paper with each new application they make. Use the patented Unequal Opportunities 'grovelmeter' to measure the levels of sycophancy to be expected from the applicants. Discard out of hand those applications which do not end with the customary terminology, i.e. 'I have the duty and pleasure to remain your humble and obedient servant'.

When you have decided on a shortlist, do not bother to inform the unsuccessful applicants that they have been rejected. Think of the postage costs involved! If anyone has been presumptuous enough to include a stamped, addressed envelope for this purpose, then steam off the stamp to offset your costs in inviting the interviewees.

The Interview

Be on the lookout from the word go for any obvious undesirables who have slipped through your shortlisting net despite all the above precautions. The trick here is to make them so uncomfortable, not to say unloved and unwanted, that they 'voluntarily' withdraw during the interview day. You can then refuse to pay them any expenses on the grounds that they have frivolously wasted your time.

On the morning of the formal interview, ask the candidates to show their teaching ability by taking a hand-picked group of your pupils for a 'demonstration lesson'. By a judicious and careful selection of pupils you can make this a modern development of the medieval trial by ordeal. Use the same group of ruffians for each candidate and put the 'undesirables' down the batting order so that your little piranha pets have had time to develop their boredom and to hone their life skills in tormenting.

Allocate a 'friendly' host for each candidate from amongst your trusties on the staff. During the guided tour of the school, each host should endeavour to operate as an *agent provocateur*. The hopefully unguarded responses of each candidate should be secretly tape-recorded for playback before the formal interviews later in the day.

On no account allow the candidates to eat on the school

premises. Suggest that this is a policy designed to give the candidates a break from the rigours of the day. If any of them asks where they can get something to eat, give deliberately unclear directions to that rather tatty tea shop a mile or so down the road. This is all part of the general initiative test and if anyone fails to return for the formal interviews, you will know that your procedures are working successfully.

Before the formal interviews begin, pass the references round the panel for a quick perusal. There's everything to be gained by soaking yourselves in a few more prejudices before you start the interrogation. Also make sure to enquire from the chair of governors whether any of the candidates is connected with the family firm in any capacity. If this should prove to be the case, there's no point in wasting any more time than you need on the others.

For each candidate, systematically adopt a different line of questioning which is likely to probe his or her weakest points. For female candidates, it is advisable to get the token woman on your panel (another relic of past phobias which should soon be discarded) to throw a fit of the vapours just before the interview starts, so that the interview panel can then be all male. This makes it a lot less embarrassing when you start to ask these females for their views on celibacy.

There should be little need to point to the sort of question in general which will trip up even the wariest of candidates who is determined to pull the wool over your eyes. One of the best approaches is to ask the candidates for their own views on equal opportunities. This usually ties them in knots.

If there are still any undesirables who have hung on up to this point, shock tactics may be called for. The patented Unequal Opportunities 'exploding coffee cup' can be a useful device on these occasions. Don't forget to make sure the coffee is at scalding temperature. If they still haven't abandoned all hope by the end of the interview, ask them in a suitably incredulous voice if they are still serious candidates for the post. If they again persist in answering in the affirmative, it's useful to have some panel members who will supply the necessary sniggers and guffaws at this point.

At the end of the interviews, it usually won't take you more than a few minutes to make up the minds of the other panellists for them, should they have not immediately supported the candidate you already have in the frame. It is, however, advisable to have some board game available at this point, because you will want to while away a half hour or so before announcing the verdict. This waiting period can often be the final successful onslaught on the nerves of the undesirables which breaks even the steeliest resolve not to depart without expenses. It also helps to soften up the successful candidate for the *coup de grâce*.

When you offer the post to the successful candidate, imply that he or she is the best of an unusually bad bunch. This is the right psychological moment to propose either a reduction in the minimum salary offered in the advertisement or some extra duties at the week-ends, or both. And welcome to the penal colony.

Getting governors to work in harmony

O NE WAY OF refreshing your understanding of the group dynamics of governors' meetings is to use a series of metaphors from the perspective of the chair, which compare them to:

The jungle

No this is not the 'nature red in tooth and claw' idea, although meetings can degenerate into that state at their extremes. What I have in mind is the fact that in the complicated ecosystem of the jungle, all the various animals have their significant roles. What you need to do is to appreciate their strengths and not deplore their deficiencies. It's no good regretting that crocodiles can't fly, that eagles can't swim under water and that fish are poor performers on dry land etc. The really skilled chairperson at governors meetings will play to the strengths of the members and compensate for their weaknesses. The thoughtful but shy Mrs Jones will need to be encouraged to put her ideas forward, while the over-confident ten-ideas-a-minute Mr Smith, will need to be restrained so that Mrs Jones can get a word in. Ideally, the restraint will be such that Mr Smith is not sent into a sulk or worse.

We rely a lot in the UK on the use of good-natured humour to oil the wheels of social interaction but, if it's the stiletto wit of cutting sarcasm which is employed, then you can expect a few dead bodies to be strewn around the jungle by the end of the meeting. While I'm on the jungle metaphor, I'm reminded that one of my favourite cartoons has a delegation of animals telling Tarzan that he's calling so many meetings that they can't get on with their various jobs. If there's insufficient business for a meeting then cancel it. If, as is more likely, there's specialist business, then delegate it to the appropriate sub-group to prepare the answers for the main meeting.

University challenge

Governors' meetings on this model are merely opportunities for individuals to demonstrate their erudition and score points off each other, and at the very worst are a series of cliques ganging up on each other. The chair should resist the role of quiz show host and quickly go back into 'team leader' mode. This should be one team with a common purpose of trying to improve the education of the children in the school, not a bunch of self-inflated egos, each one trying desperately to assert its own intellectual superiority. Service to others is the key, not self-aggrandisement.

The group therapy session

All meetings have elements of this. Egos will need to be massaged, paranoia will have to be assuaged and megalomania will need to be curbed. This is saving the National Health Service a lot of much needed cash, which is fine, but do remember that this is not the main purpose of governors' meetings. You are not the outpatients' section of your local psychiatric ward. Your job is to focus the various drives of your members on the task of improving the education of children. Their paranoias should focus on the very real threats which reduced budgets will pose for the school. Who needs imaginary persecutors in times like these?

The battleground

This is one stage worse than 'university challenge', because you've got a potential civil war on your hands with warring factions determined to take no prisoners. Tip for chairperson, the one who is holding up a pathetic white handkerchief of a flag and dodging the bullets in no-man's land: there's nothing like the threat of a common enemy at the gates to unite the feuding citizenry within the walls. Fortunately there's a very obvious candidate for Public Enemy Number One at present and, if you can fix all eyes upon this, you should soon be marching into battle with a united platoon armed with a common purpose.

The theatre

Every governors' meeting is a stage, and all the men and women merely players, to paraphrase the bard (who also knew a thing or two about group dynamics). As an alternative venue to the local amateur dramatic society, your meetings may be the less attractive proposition, but that won't dissuade the dedicated thespians from doing their turns. Don't give them free auditions. It is a forlorn hope that they will become tired of hearing themselves speak if you let them go on long enough. They are having a lifelong love affair with their own voices and they are convinced the rest of the world can't get enough of them. Focus their talents. Arrange opportunities for them to make impassioned diatribes from the town hall steps against the draining away of the nation's lifeblood of education. Now that's a setting they will see as worthy of their best performances, with or without the presence of television camera crews.

The orchestra

Let's end on an upbeat note with the harmonious tones of various instrumental players all blending into a virtuoso performance. Individually, each has his or her own skills, but working together in a disciplined way under a gifted conductor it's amazing how brilliant the combined efforts can be. Now there's an ideal worth aiming for in governors' meetings.

Flattery will get you almost anywhere

I HAVE WRITTEN elsewhere about headteachers as 'Administrators', 'Managers' and 'Leaders', pointing to the distinctions between these categories. I have also argued that although any one headteacher may at different times act in all three roles, the likelihood is that you will be able to identify your head as predominantly behaving in one preferred style. The question I now want to try to answer is how are you best going to manage your head once you've worked out which kind of head he or she is? (For heads themselves, the spin-off benefit may be to alert them to some of the tricks their teachers may be employing as a means of head-control.)

I usually try to avoid blinding readers with academic references, but in this case there may be a few remaining idealists who require some convincing evidence, beyond the seductive persuasiveness of my prose alone, that flattery will get you almost anywhere. Two research findings in particular have added more confirmation to the wealth of evidence that wheedling your way into the boss's good books may be the quickest way up the ladder of success.

The first research study had the suitably impressive title of 'The

Impact of the Frequency of Ingratiation on the Performance Evaluation of Bank Personnel', and was written up by John D. Watt of Kansas State University in *The Journal of Psychology, Vol.127 No.2*. He concluded that it was the more sycophantic of the bank staff who were likely to get favourable appraisals from their bosses and to gain good promotions ratings. The second publication was *The Role of Subordinate Performance and Ingratiation in Leader-Member Exchanges*, by R. Deluga and J. Perry of Bryant College, Smithfield, Rhode Island, USA, which reached broadly similar conclusions about the efficacy of flattery in the workplace in general. In the USA, they even have now the 'American Measure of Ingratiatory Behaviours in Organizational Settings' or MIBOS for short (I kid you not!), which measures the frequency of 'creep' tactics used by employees.

The downsides to crawling to your boss, according to studies such as these, are that it may reduce your job satisfaction, and woe betide you if your fellow crawlers latch on to the fact that you are busting all known creep norms in your ingratiatory drive for success. In school you must, therefore, avoid at all costs being seen by your colleagues as the head's 'trusty'. From time to time, you should be seen to disagree publicly with the head on some suitably trivial issue (on which, of course, you will allow him or her to talk you round in private later, thus confirming your ultimate ability to see reason and the head's renowned ability to sell ice-cream to Eskimos).

Agent provocateur

The danger with joining in the staff room criticism of the head as a cover for your private acts of ingratiation is that this latest gripe session amongst the unwary may have been set up by an *agent provocateur* on the staff, who is even now compiling a hit list of names for the head in question. As for job satisfaction, this need only concern those who are trailing along with them some outdated baggage labelled 'honour' or 'integrity' or the like. These concepts may have had their place in the writings of French and Spanish dramatists in the sixteenth century, but never forget that they, too, were appealing to the inflated self-images of their patrons.

One William Shakespeare was no slouch in the courtier-to-monarch ingratiation stakes either, where laying it on with a trowel was (and is still?) considered *de rigueur,* but he did have the unfortunate habit in this respect of being unable to avoid telling it like it was from time to time.

There are, of course, heads who will argue that the very thought of such behaviour would never even be entertained by the teachers in their schools, and there are no doubt others who would argue that the last people they would wish to employ are sycophants. The latter heads might care to reflect on yet more immortal lines from Sam Goldwyn, that well known proponent of workplace democracy, who is reported as saying, in a time long before political correctness had to be considered, that 'he did not wish to be surrounded by yes-men. He wanted all his employees to tell him the truth even if it was at the cost of their jobs!' The former heads, who probably rank very highly on *The British Measures of Gullibility and Self-Delusion in High Places* (a rating scale I am about to patent), might like to produce the research evidence that indicates that their teachers are significantly different from the workforce in general in these respects.

So what are the most skilful and tried and tested ingratiation tactics? Imitation stands out above all others. If your head is predominantly the Bureaucrat, then you should be forever sending memos in triplicate to all and sundry, preferably pointing to the dangers involved in taking any kind of positive action on any issue whatsoever. If your head is the Manager type, then you should obtain a copy of *How To Bluff Your Way To Success Through Management Jargon*. (If such a text doesn't exist, by the way, then it ought to. Indeed, I can't imagine what else many of the managers I come into contact with could otherwise have been consulting.) A few appropriately dropped references to the advantages of cost-benefit analysis or zero-based budgeting should be enough in any case. Be careful, however, in case the Manager in question actually approaches you in private to pick your brains on these issues. This may require a reading of the *Advanced Bluffers' Guide*, although there is a very real danger here that your head may be using this as his or her own working bible. This could lead to some amusing but potentially perilous dialogues.

Knots

If your head is the Leader, then adopt a 'can do' approach, leaving around the place some telling evidence that you have been cutting Gordian knots left, right and centre. You will probably succeed in leaving a few gashes on your colleagues as you swing your Gordian knot cutter around, so if the blood on the carpet isn't enough for the head, the cries of the victims are sure to reach the Führerbunker, where they will be taken as evidence that you are not only cutting knots but also breaking eggs in the preparation of one more organisational omelette (another metaphor beloved of the 'can do' head).

This raises the issue of how to ensure that your subtler messages are getting through to the head. The problem with direct flattery is that there could possibly be a few heads who might recognise this currying of favour for what it is and make a public show of despising anyone considered to be fawning upon them. To guard against this admittedly highly unlikely eventuality, you should always use the indirect approach (as the wise old French duke observed many years ago, those who claim to be repelled by flattery are probably only rejecting the particularly clumsy style of the flatterer rather than flattery itself). Hence, as indicated above, the real beauty of imitation as the most indirect and possibly the insincerest form of flattery.

Other indirect approaches are also worth a try. If you have been able to blow the cover of the *agent provocateur* on the staff, then you will have a sure conduit for your flattery. It is essential to locate the head's spies for these purposes, because they will be the ones who will best whisper your praises in his or her ear. Some whisperers will be as difficult to discover as you are yourself in the undercover role you have adopted. Others tend to be overlooked for the usual reasons of snobbery in the English caste system. Those who ignore on such grounds the whispering potential of such key figures as the caretaker or the school secretary do so at their own peril.

Lonely at the top

Heads are lonely figures. Any member of the teaching staff obviously acting as a confidant(e) is, as already indicated, one of the head's cronies in the eyes of all the other teachers and almost certainly perceived by them as a member of the inner clique who are 'in the know'. For this reason, heads are likely to avoid being seen regularly walking around the school talking to particular members of the teaching staff. But nobody bats an eyelid when they see the caretaker wandering around with the head. Indeed, strolls with the caretaker are an excellent cover for managing by walking about. If you think that all the head and the caretaker ever discuss is the state of the school boilers, you are almost certainly mistaken.

A far more obvious 'boss's nark', and one never likely to be overlooked, will be a deputy figure who is bound to be a member of the magic circle. Such individuals have it built into their job descriptions that they will be 'the eyes and ears of the head'. This is tantamount to affixing a label on their backs marked 'official informant', or 'head's grass', as it is known in the trade. The little local difficulty here is that the deputy is all too familiar with attempts to use him or her as the conveyer of compliments to the chief. It might, therefore, have a pay-off value to heap praises on aspects of the head's performance that the deputy may consider have a certain rarity value. Deputies will be well aware that bureaucratic heads may harbour certain Walter Mitty-like delusions of their prowess as pro-active leaders. The odd spot of recognition of heretofore hidden derring-do qualities on the part of the bureaucratic head may be carried by the deputy as rapidly as the good news from Ghent to Aix.

The final indirect flattery possibility to which you would do well to give serious consideration is the establishment of a flattery cabal. If you can find two or three others in a fellow state of lowliness who are also viewing it as a potential young ambition's ladder, then why not form a secret mutual admiration society? The one club rule is that whenever the names of Jane or Fred crop up in idle staff room conversation, you go over the top in praise of their many virtues. Pour on the old oil, as Bertie Wooster would put it. This will be so startling a reversal of normal procedures that the gossips (who should never be confused with the whisperers because of the profligate way in which the former disperse their information) will have the message around the staff in general in no time at all. The whisperers will take it from there as far as those in high places are concerned. But if Fred and Jane are sufficiently trustworthy, they are doing just the same for you. When, in later years (and they shouldn't be that much later), you are all three celebrating your first headships and drinking a toast to the secret society that has brought you so far, don't for a moment think of disbanding. There are still plenty of rungs on the ladder left to climb.

The rumour mill

ANY HEADS worth their salt and pepper are well aware that if they want to communicate something to their staffs in as short a time as possible and in such a way as to make the latter pay maximum attention to the message, the most efficacious method is to whisper it to someone in utter and total confidence. It can then be guaranteed that the word will be round the staff like wildfire, with individuals hanging on to every syllable (thus demonstrating once again that the phrase: 'your secret is safe with me' is up there along with 'your cheque is in the post' in the ranks of all time greatest lies).

They can also guarantee that, if their communication is a rebuke directed against some member of staff or other, there will be some colleagues down the line only too delighted to pass the message on to the individual concerned (usually by means of pinning it to the stiletto which they then proceed to slip between the unfortunate one's unguarded ribs).

The shock/horror effects will be all the sharper, however mild the original message, because the latter will, as if by black magic, have become truly wicked by the end of this 'Chinese whispers' exercise. A further advantage of this technique is that it can later be denied, if necessary, that any official communication to this effect ever took place. Certainly the original confidant(e) is not going to put his or her head above the parapet by alleging publicly that the head whispered the rumour in the first place. Recipients of the bad word who got the aspersion only somewhere along the chain will be simply unaware of the original source, although they may harbour shrewd suspicions.

Governments in the UK have, of course, developed this technique into a minor art form, even dignifying their selective and unattributable leaks by processes such as 'the official parliamentary lobby system'. None of this, of course, stops individual ministers of government becoming suitably indignant and irate if anyone else should leak information which they do not wish to see in the public domain. This then becomes the subject of an official enquiry, at the end of which some unfortunate individual who has been foolish enough to trust in the integrity of some newspaper editor or other may end up in clink.

Part of the problem, as far as heads are also concerned, is that they have no monopoly of the rumour mill. Even the lowliest NQT can bring grist to be ground into calumny. However, the verb can, as ever, be conjugated to indicate clearly that what may be acceptable – nay, laudable – conduct on your own part is far from acceptable in the behaviour of others. Hence: I network, you gossip; s/he wastes his/her time in idle chit chat, we inform appropriate sources; you leak, they are traitors.

Art form

The art of spreading rumour and remaining fireproof is, however, even more complex an art form than I have indicated so far. For example, let us take the case of a middle manager (whom we shall call Bill), who has whispered a calumny about someone of higher rank in the organisational pecking order than himself (Jean), and is then tipped the wink that the person to whom he has whispered the rumour (Fred) is already hawking the story around as evidence of Bill's disloyalty and worse? Sooner or later, Bill knows this is going to reach Jean, the person against whom his rumour was originally aimed.

Before this happens, he has to get in his pre-emptive strike. He sorrowfully goes to his own line manager and says he is terribly worried about Fred. Bill was having what he thought was a perfectly normal conversation with him the other day 'about some of the burning issues which concern all of us in the organisation', and it was quite clear that Fred was constantly putting very unkind words about Jean into Bill's totally innocent mouth. It was very much the 'don't you think this or that about the way Jean is behaving lately?' approach. Bill resolutely refused to agree with this, of course, but short of actually being offensive to Fred, it was impossible to shut him up. So it was hard for Bill not to feel that he had been made part of something with which he wanted to have nothing to do.

This puts the senior management into something of a quandary. If they are naive enough, Bill may have managed to convince them of his own loyalty and of the extreme perfidy of Fred, who will only confirm the truth of Bill's story by retelling the original rumour-mongering to management either directly or indirectly. If they have any sense, however, the senior management will trust neither Bill nor Fred, but they still will not know for certain where the blame lies this time around. Either way, Bill is better off than he was before he launched his counter-offensive.

A very well known use of rumour is for someone to let it be known that they are in the frame for a job elsewhere but don't really want to leave an organisation where he or she had been perfectly happy until this opportunity came along. (This game can only be played by those who are certain their bosses would not be delighted to see the back of them!) When the rumour gets back to senior management, the latter may just see its way to offering either internal promotion or an increased salary, or both, as a means of preventing the person in question being enticed away by the competition. As already suggested, this is a card to be played with caution and it must never be over-played.

This is indicative of rumour-mongering in general, where timing is of the essence and style and direction of delivery are critical factors in ensuring successful outcomes. For this is a high risk strategy where, once the incontrovertible proof is revealed of who is the real meddler behind the grapevine disinformation, the heavens will probably descend on the double-dyed villain concerned. It's all very well using Desdemona's handkerchief to slander Cassio, but it could become conclusive proof of your own treachery if you have been foolish enough to count on your own wife's silence.

Motive for malignancy

I have never understood, by the way, why Iago is accused by some drama critics of 'motiveless malignancy'. Othello passed him over for promotion, didn't he? In my time, I've seen reactions to similar events in the world of education which make Iago seem like a model of tolerant moderation by comparison. Indeed, the recurrent sharp pains in my shoulder blades could be caused by any one of a number of unpromoted people who are given to sticking pins into wax dolls.

Thinking of Iago, I am reminded that one of the main purposes of organisational rumour-mongering is to discredit your rivals and competitors. Heads should be very wary of 'chance remarks', from whatever source, which appear to be sympathetic to the weaknesses of their middle managers. Examples of the kind of thing I have in mind are: 'pity about old Jill's drink problem'; 'best to go easy on Sam for a while – his private life's in a bit of a mess at the moment'; 'I really don't see that Joan's sexual tendencies have anything to do with her professional life', etc.

On no account should you probe your informant about any such remark casting obscure doubt on the competence of, for example, your deputy, Jack. This will usually provoke a sudden clamming up, which is ostensibly intended to demonstrate the essential integrity of the whisperer, but which is really designed to make you suspect the situation is infinitely more sinister than anything which has been indicated so far.

In any case, you can bet the rumour was planted a long way up the chain by another of the middle managers who fancies being lined up for that deputy head vacancy when old Jack retires. This is bound to occur soon, 'since it's so sad to see what can happen to you when you hang on to the job too long.' In these days of increasingly impatient young men and women in negative equity this is a nobblingly ageist line which can be applied to anyone over the age of 40. For counters to these gambits by young people in a hurry, please consult my forthcoming treatise entitled *The Wrinklies' Guide To Keeping Young Whippersnappers In Their Place.* It isn't only a woman's place which is 'in the wrong'. Thurber may have been sexist, but I am thinking of starting a new trend in 'youthism', which is the reverse of the usual form of ageism.

My own experience over the years suggests that the rumour mill of any organisation will continue to grind on come what may, but the more secretive the organisation, the faster the mill wheel will race.

A lot of the rumour-mongering that goes on stems from the insecurity of the information-poor, and from a desire on the part of a few of them to create a false appearance of information-richness. It boosts their self-esteem to create the impression that they are in the know and 'have friends in higher places'. The odd thing about this, to my eyes at least, is that it doesn't seem to matter too much to this particular breed, or for that matter to the recipients of their information, if they are peddling duff gen for around 80% to 90% of the time. They only need to strike lucky roughly once in ten times for that to be the gusher which is long remembered. This may be linked to gamblers' happy memories of their 'big wins', which seem to blot out any recollection of what in many cases must be their even bigger losses (or why are bookmakers so well dressed?). Perhaps there's a case for a new organisation called 'Rumour-mongers Anonymous'?

School for scandal

THERE WAS some bewilderment expressed by officials at the Department of Trade and Industry when complaints were directed at a booklet entitled *Marketing Your Business*, produced on their behalf by a private consultancy (source: *The Independent*, 4 and 5 November 1994). Apparently, some of those who read this Crown-copyright manual actually objected to receiving advice about the dirty tricks they should employ when trying to gain some competitive edge over their business rivals. Dubbing this booklet a 'Cheats' Charter', one company boss (who asked not to be named) said: 'I'm absolutely appalled. It seems as if to succeed in this world you have to lose all your scruples and morals.'

The DTI failed to understand why this outrage should have been expressed over a few handy tips such as going through competitors' rubbish bins, lying about whom you represent and befriending secretaries to rival firms 'with access to photocopiers'.

Even some unnamed civil servant expressed a worry that a 'cheating culture appears to have been actually advocated by the government', thus revealing that there are still some unworldly officials closeted away in the hidden depths of Whitehall who have become as blind as moles to what has been happening in the wider political environment for this past decade and more. Unless, of course, the art of irony is being nurtured and preserved as part of English Heritage by Sir Humphrey Appleby and his fellow mandarins.

I can nevertheless fully understand the main reason for the general bewilderment amongst the less naive bureaucrats at the DTI. They must feel that their minor venture into promulgating the art of chicanery is a mere molehill beside the veritable sleaze mountain they can observe from their office windows. What has not been known until now, for example, is that this booklet is but a pale shadow of a secret manual issued by the DfE only to an entrepreneurial elite of headteachers and chairs of governing bodies.

I have managed to obtain a copy of this booklet, entitled *Marketing Your School and Devil take The Hindmost,* by taking a close personal interest in the affairs of one of the secretaries in Sanctuary Buildings. This charming young lady was kind enough to send me a copy of the tract in a plain brown envelope, and so I am now in a position to bring the advice of the DfE to a much wider public. To whet your appetite, I have extracted a few paragraphs from this latest production, which I am sure would be a potential best-seller should the DfE decide to issue it more generally:

'It is essential that you keep yourself fully informed about your competitor schools' current activities and, more importantly, their future plans. No potential source of information should be neglected. Put in tenders for school cleaning and rubbish collection under such letter headings as 'Kleen You Out plc.' These will need to be very low tenders indeed to undercut the many other firms in this market who are employing 'job seekers' on starvation wages. Never forget that you have the incomparable advantage of having a pool of labour that can be employed on such tasks for no wages at all. Indeed, once the work is under way, you can present it in the school prospectus as yet another example of the splendidly innovative projects you have devised to introduce tomorrow's citizens to the world of work today.

'Encourage the budding entrepreneurs among your young

charges to set up school companies in this way, and to act as employers of those of their fellow pupils less well endowed with managerial acumen but perfectly capable of learning invaluable lessons in the art of daily survival in the workplace. You will, of course, also have work gangs operating on sorting out the material which has been collected on these cleaning operations. The nimble fingers of young females are particularly well adapted to such work. Much useful income can be derived from selling off some of the by-products of these enterprises.'

Gathering intelligence

'The elite among the 'sorters' brigades' will be the intelligence gathering corps. They will be principally employed in piecing back together and interpreting any documents which your rival establishments have been careless enough not to consign to the incinerators. You are unlikely to have to run specialist courses in code breaking for such youngsters, as few educational outfits have had your foresight and are unlikely to be operating the latest state-of-the-art encoding machines. Naturally, you will claim, to any parents who happen to hear whispers of the nature of these activities, that data collection and information gathering are highly prized life skills in this new knowledge society. It should easily be possible to get such work accredited in any case, and the carrot of GNVQs should be dangled before pupils and parents alike.

'Should any parent actually wander by accident into the 'Enigma Sheds', and wonder about the slogans plastered around the walls to the effect that careless talk costs lives, etc, you will immediately claim that the posters accompanying these slogans may appear a trifle lurid and brutal but the world has moved on since their day and you are attempting to create an authentic atmosphere of commercial warfare in a global market.

'Other pupils may need to work alongside staff on the telephone cold calling section. Deception capabilities of the highest quality will be needed to convince your rival schools that they are being contacted by media representatives, the local gendarmerie, or even MI6 or Special Branch, etc. Your staff will welcome these opportunities to hone their 'selling' skills, as they will all be employed on extremely short term contracts, with the daily threat hanging over them of a return to the timeshare salt mines from whence they came.

'*La crème de la crème* of these operatives may be sent on personal 'search and destroy' missions to enemy territory. However, they must understand that, should their cover be blown, you will disown them if they are foolish enough to claim that they are in your employ. The more honourable of them may, under such circumstances, use the standard issue cyanide tablets concealed in the hollow teeth you will thoughtfully have provided for such eventualities, but in these disloyal times you should not count on it. It is wise, therefore, to infiltrate more than one agent at a time into the enemy camp.

'As in the renowned Polish police force under the former Communist regime, agents should ideally operate in threes. You will recall that in Warsaw, the explanation for this was that one policeman could read, the second could write and the third was required to keep an eye on the two intellectuals. In your case, no individual agent should be aware of the identity of the other agents operating on his or her territory until it is absolutely necessary.'

Infiltrating the enemy camp

'In one classic case on our files, School X had pulled the master stroke of having infiltrated not only the school caretaker and the head of the modern languages department into School Y, unbeknown to each other, but the headteacher of School Y was actually an undercover agent of School X who had been sent there as a 'sleeper' many years previously. She had worked her way up the promotion ladder so assiduously, however, that when the time came to activate her, she refused to recommend school closure and had, therefore, to be eliminated, along with the head of modern languages, who had also gone native. It was an act of the greatest ingenuity on the part of the 'caretaker' to make their deaths look like the suicide pact of a pair of drugged and star-crossed lovers, and the resulting scandal resulted in the desired school closure after all.

'You should also have learned some useful lessons from British Airways' apologies to Richard Branson's Virgin Airline for their 'dirty tricks' campaign involving the poaching of passengers and obtaining of confidential information (the most important lesson, of course, being not to be caught red handed!). Now that catchment areas are no longer sacrosanct, you can try hiring a fleet of luxury coaches to cruise around the more salubrious parts of your rivals' territory, carrying suitably emblazoned banners proclaiming the wonders of your own emporium and the free gifts obtainable on enrolment. Heads of rivals' feeder schools may be induced to act as poachers on your behalf if you follow the time-honoured soccer practices of bunging them used fivers in buff envelopes in service stations on nearby motorways. Be on your guard, however, against hidden cameras and double-crosses from your 'business associates'.

'Disinformation is also useful to counter your rivals' own surveillance tactics. Be sure to place in your local rags regular advertisements of the innovative new courses you intend to introduce into your school's curricular portfolio. Liberally scatter acronyms such as RSAF, GNVQ, HLS, FSVOC, etc. across the column inches. It will be money well spent. The key point here is not only that you have absolutely no intention whatsoever of running courses leading to these qualifications, but that most of them are totally fictitious, despite their apparent superficial plausibility. This should drive some of your competitor heads into early graves. Some of them will lash their hirelings into constructing rival courses, thereby increasing the breakdown rates amongst their staffs, while others will drive themselves to distraction trying to find details of the non-existent courses for which you have invented acronyms. Meanwhile, you will have gained a spurious reputation for being go-ahead and innovative amongst the parents in the locality.'

And so on and so on. No head can afford to be without this classic text for our times – it's up to you to seek the appropriate individual(s) to cultivate. How do you think I got the list in the first place? Alternatively, you might submit a tender for the cleaning contract, but I warn you that you are highly unlikely to be able to undercut the existing contract with 'HellHole SqueakyKleen plc.'

Have you ever tried doing a spellcheck on your wordprocessor for 'Hellawell', by the way?

Twenty ways to kill a new idea

The guide for the headteacher from hell now offers the definitive checklist for the extermination of new ideas from members of staff. Just in case there may be some heads out there who are actually naive enough to think it might be a good idea to encourage staff ideas, I suggest that they think again. New ideas in general are dangerous. Government think tanks are actually set up to generate new ideas, and look what a mess they have got you and your fellow sufferers into in recent years. You've had enough problems implementing (or pretending to implement) the latest political wheezes from Whitehall each term, without having to make changes proposed by your own staff.

New ideas from staff are messy. They invariably disrupt the smooth-running personal routine which you have taken years to achieve. However innocuous they may appear to be at first sight, you can bet your petty cash that they will prevent you from continuing to fly on automatic pilot at some point, and they may also need more than just petty cash finance. Worse, they may require thought on your part, and you know how that hurts your head. Some of them may even demand action by you, which is precisely what you have been seeking to avoid at all costs before your retirement day. So what can you do to counteract the new idea?

1. Ignore it. If it appears in memo form, then lose the memo. Remember that the waste bin is the head's best friend. If it appears as a spoken remark in a meeting, pretend not to have heard it. There is every chance that it will die from neglect. Think of it as a sacrifice you are offering up to whichever gods you think will thrive on a diet of still-born ideas.

2. If it reappears, either in written or spoken form, you could try ignoring it again, but you will almost certainly have to take some action or other to kill it eventually. A first step is to suggest that this is not the right time for it. The more flattering alternative is to suggest that the ideas merchant is years in advance of current thinking on the subject. 'This is a really creative idea, but the parents/governors/public in general aren't ready for this yet.' (There is, incidentally, an exact formula by which to ascertain when the date (X) will be propitious for a creative new idea of this kind. This can be stated as $X = Y + 1$, where Y is the date of your retirement.) The less flattering alternative is to suggest that s/he's already missed that tide in the affairs of men and women which Bill Shakespeare thought it was so important to catch. 'This might have washed in the 60s, but the world has moved on since then.'

3. This latter approach can be reinforced by the suggestion that it was tried in the school before his or her time and it didn't work then, so you can't see why it should work now. 'We tried that in '73 and it was a washout.' A further refinement of this ploy is to link it with the name of either some incompetent, or someone hated by the staff (or preferably, someone who was both hated and incompetent), who has now conveniently left the school to avoid being tarred and feathered. The suggestion that this legend in his or her own lifetime is rumoured to have harboured similar intentions will be more than enough to scupper the idea.

4. Alternatively, the fact that the idea has never been tried in the school before can be an equally damning condemnation of it, e.g. 'If this idea were as good as you claim, we'd have tried it long before now,' or, 'This is a novel suggestion but it might set a dangerous precedent.' (Any new idea is, by definition, a dangerous precedent.) It is not recommended that you should try an approach along the lines of: 'You can't teach an old dog new tricks.' This may encourage notions of getting rid of the old dog.

5. There are similar dangers in suggesting that if only eyes were kept open it would be clear that this sort of thing has been going on all the time, albeit covertly and under another name. 'You're trying to teach your grandmother how to suck eggs.' This may be an encouragement to the euthanasia brigade.

6. A reliable standby on almost all occasions is to suggest that, despite the obvious merits of the idea, there simply isn't the time to implement it. A few covering remarks to the effect that you are only too well aware of the crippling burdens your staff are working under may even help to promote the notion that you are a caring manager. 'If it weren't for all these totally unreasonable deadlines set by this excuse for a government, we might be able to do something about it.'

7. There will be the occasional smart Alec who has already done some research to the effect that the idea is already up and running at old Fred's school down the road. The standard counter to this is that it might work in Fred's school but that's only because it's bigger/smaller/more progressive/less progressive ... and so on. etc. But you've grasped the basic notion of the counter by now. Your place is different. Nobody can deny that. The distinctive characteristics of your establishment mean that any transplant from another culture will only lead to tissue rejection.

8. On the other hand, why should you want to develop new home-grown ideas when everything is working so smoothly already? 'We've been doing it this way for donkey's years and it hasn't let us down yet.' 'If it ain't bust don't fix it.' 'We're doing OK as it is and we don't want to rock the boat.'

9. Another approach is to suggest that you are right behind the idea but you know the governors would never wear it. If only you had a free hand! This ploy was used to great effect by one Joseph Vissarionovich Djugashvili, or Stalin as he preferred to be known, when negotiating the division of Europe at Yalta. 'Oh yes, I think that's a very good suggestion for Poland's Western border, but that damned Politburo back in Moscow will never stand for it.' If Uncle Joe could get away, as he did, with the highly implausible scenario that he was going to care a tinker's cuss about the views of the Politburo, then you can certainly use the governors with impunity as bogeymen and women. Don't go overboard about the perils of treading on the toes of the powers that be, however, because you might be open to allegations of trimming or cowardice. This was not a problem for Stalin, who had more scope for dealing with troublemakers than you have.

10. If you think the excuse of the governors in this respect is wearing a bit thin, then try other potential blockers. 'This is fine, but the staff will never live with it,' is unfortunately open to cross checking by the ideas merchant, as is 'But the unions would never accept it.' This line has become increasingly implausible with the rapid decline of union power, but the average teacher may still think that UNISON has some punching power on behalf of the non-teaching staff.

11. 'It's contrary to LEA policy' has its advantages, as nobody knows what LEA policy is on anything and you are, therefore, unlikely to be doubted. On the other hand, this line is also losing its impact as the grip of the local 'office' weakens, but it's still a better holding line than: 'I think we ought to sleep on this one for a while.' This suggests that you go about your work in a somnambulistic fashion. It may also prompt the stubborn ideas merchant (and boy, *can* they be stubborn) to return some days later to enquire whether your slumbers have been sufficient for you now to pass judgement. As I hope you have begun to gather by now, the whole point of the exercise is somehow to imply that the issue is outside your own control. If only you had the freedom! 'You're absolutely right, but . . .' is a surefire formula to which I am sure you can fill in a host of imaginative sentence endings.

12. Some of your ideas merchants may have a soft heart (but don't count on it) which you can use to your advantage. So try something along the lines of 'Yes, but this is really going to put old Jill out of a job. I don't see what else she could do after all these years.' This may wring the withers of some of the more sensitive of your staff, and for others you could add the line, 'and she wouldn't be the last to go by a long chalk.' Said with the requisite steely glint and the right amount of eye contact, this should carry the message that the ideas merchants are signing their own death warrants with this one. (Budding actors should study the eye technique of Clint Eastwood as he entreats those he refers to as 'punks' to go ahead and make his day. This slit-eyed gaze is known as the gunslinger's stare. Cultivate it.) This should bring the insensitive in line with the sensitive on this issue.

13. On the other hand, you could imply that the idea will take up far more resources than the school could ever have available in a month of Sundays. 'We haven't enough staff/money/equipment, etc.' is a little on the lame side. A more challenging approach is to say something like: 'Yes, this is an interesting way of diverting our limited resources, but you will have to show me which budget heading I should raid to find the necessary funds.' You might even go on to propose a particular heading which you know to be very dear indeed to the heart of the proponent of the idea. This should be a certain kiss of death to the idea, and you will never hear of it again.

14. For the more idle of your ideas merchants, you can put the following argument to good use: 'This looks interesting but it'll need a lot more flesh on the bones. If you really want me to pursue this matter, perhaps you could do some further research/investigation and produce a paper for me on the subject. Don't go beyond ten sides of A4.' With a bit of luck, there will be a fervent hope that you will now forget all about it. You will graciously

47

live up to this expectation.

15. Suggest that the idea will require staff to undergo considerable retraining, starting with the ideas merchant. 'I don't think the staff are really ready for this just yet. We've nobody with the kind of skills your idea would require for successful implementation.' There are bound to be some mind-numbingly boring aspects of the implementation as well, and you could suggest that the ideas person is just the member of staff to be retrained for these exciting possibilities.

16. Argue that there could well be unforeseen complications which might lead to the idea having all kinds of outcomes which were entirely unintended. As nobody can possibly foresee all the outcomes of new ideas, you are on very safe ground here. A hint of menace that one of the unintended outcomes could be a blockage to an otherwise promising career might help to drive the point home.

17. Some ideas persons can be flattered by the line that while it's an intriguingly ingenious idea in theory, you have doubts (based, of course, on your superior experience and wisdom) whether it would ever work out as well in practice. Imply that if only all the other dolts on the staff had the insight of the two of you, then the implementation would, of course, be a doddle.

18. Others can be threatened by a statement to the effect that although you, yourself, can see that the idea was put forward for the best possible motives, there are other, baser souls on the staff who will think that this is a self-serving careerist proposal with politically opportunist overtones.

19. In meetings which you are chairing, it may be possible to kill the idea by ridicule. 'That's a bit too clever for old-timers like us,' should put young whippersnappers in their place, and this will go down well with the old lags around the table who were beginning to get a bit worried by the competition. Even more economical is the whispered aside that everyone can hear which conveys amused astonishment that anything so footling should ever have been put forward. A suitably raised eyebrow is an appropriate accompaniment to the aside. The brighter the proposed innovation, the better this works. Such an approach is rumoured to have done for Mozart, so it should certainly work in your school.

20. If you're getting tired of deploying arguments to kill ideas, then there's always the possibility of setting up a committee that you know will kill it for you. The trick here is to place on it some staff who have long-standing scores to settle with the idea's main protagonist. The merits or otherwise of the idea won't then come into question. Your choice of committee members should ensure that there is sufficient blood on the carpet by the end of their deliberations to make any positive recommendations highly unlikely (but do take care that your placemen and women don't have even greater scores to settle with you).

The myth of the female manager

A TRADITIONAL LINE of writers on women in management is that women who aspire to managerial positions in education have to adopt 'male' or 'masculine' characteristics to achieve career success. These characteristics have been variously typified as toughness, resilience, rationality in problem-solving, competitiveness and power seeking, etc.

Male managers who others (most commonly, of course, the argument runs, other men) see as 'good promotion material' are argued to be, for example, decisive, aggressive, independent, self-confident and, the most general and perhaps most vacuous criterion of all, strong.

The masculine characteristics of organisations are often presented as those in which there are vertical and hierarchical power structures, where individuals compete against each other on win-lose models, where strategic (note the military metaphors) decisions are taken in an analytical and unemotional organisation and where there is a high level of control.

Some have argued that the modern forms of bureaucratic organisation, seen by many as the most typical feature of developed societies in the twentieth century, are inherently ill-matched with the nurturing, expressive and inter-personal orientations typically associated with women.

Thus Max Weber's classic early formulation of the criteria of bureaucracy included 'a spirit of formalistic impersonality – without hatred or passion, but hence without love or affection.' Other writers have argued it is precisely because women are obliged to take on these non-feminine characteristics, if they are to succeed, that relatively few of them put themselves forward for promotion into managerial positions.

Those who do are argued typically to experience a constant dilemma of being expected to be 'masculine' in their organisational behaviour while being stigmatised as having lost their femininity in the process. This role conflict has led to constant stress, it is argued, for those women managers unwilling to follow the out and out masculine role model (perhaps we could label this the female manager's 'feel-bad factor'?). Indeed, it has been suggested that the women least likely to experience stress in the traditional managerial role are those who were of a 'masculine' orientation to start with. Hence the joke, current in the early 1970s, to the effect that Mrs Thatcher was the only 'man' in Edward Heath's cabinet.

Dilemmas

I find it interesting that some women managers appear to have internalised some of these judgements. One of the very few women ever to become a university vice-chancellor in the UK, Baroness Perry, was quoted as follows, at the time of her resignation, on the dilemmas facing women managers in education:

'We have learned to rely too heavily on the skills of compliance and of pleasing others; being liked is most important to us. For a woman to pull out of the crowd and to move up the ladder of management responsibility is extremely difficult. I have never forgotten one woman head of a school commenting on how lonely she felt in her job and saying to me: "The worst experience of a head is to walk along the corridor and hear the laughter coming from the staff room, knowing that if you enter the room it would stop".'

I personally do not accept the validity of her comment on the loneliness of the headteacher's job being worse for females than males. As a very young lecturer visiting schools in the Yorkshire Dales, I was struck very early on by the fact that male headteachers much older than myself (and they were male, more often than not) would pour out their managerial (and out of school) troubles to me in a manner which I initially found disconcerting.

I soon tumbled to the fact that it had little if anything to do with any 'father confessor' characteristics they detected in me, and was much more a testimony to the effect that they were occupationally lonely individuals for whom any outsider's visit was an opportunity to 'unload' in ways they could never do with their own staff or pupils.

What I do find significant in Baroness Perry's comment is that she perceives women as more likely to be lonely in their managerial roles and more wanting to be liked than men would be in similar positions. However, I may add, in the light of my later comments, that I do not share this latter perspective either. I have known an awful lot of male managers who courted popularity at all costs.

If we accept, however, for the sake of argument, that these are more feminine than masculine characteristics, they might once have been viewed by management writers as inherent weaknesses in the female manager, but this is often no longer the case with such commentators. The current fashion in management writing is to argue that such 'feminine' characteristics are increasingly desirable in the managers of the 'learning organisations' of the future.

Leadership needs

In his seminal book on these learning organisations, *The Fifth Discipline*, Peter Senge has written of the new leadership needs of the institutions as follows:

'In a learning organisation, leaders are designers, stewards and teachers. They are responsible for building organisations where people continually expand their capabilities to understand complexity, clarify vision and improve shared mental models – that is they are responsible for learning.'

Other writers have concluded that the early socialisation of women makes them better equipped than men to lead and develop such organisations. It is argued that women are less likely than men to go for 'win-lose' solutions in areas of conflict and are much more prone to seek outcomes in which every participant can gain some satisfaction (so-called 'win-win' negotiations).

Women, so the argument runs, are more likely than men to wish to foster harmonious inter-personal relations in organisations which facilitate collaborative team-working approaches to problem-solving. The skills of mentoring, coaching and helping others to learn are considered to be in high demand in the learning organisation, and women are seen as more likely to possess such skills.

A new wave of women managers is now envisaged as breaking on to the organisational shore and bringing with it a more caring approach than the traditional masculine one; an approach which encourages consensus-building and participation by others.

My problem with all this is that it seems to stereotype male and female characteristics, and it leaves us in danger of making assumptions about the likely behaviour of those in positions of power in educational organisations which are not borne out by my experience and that of others of my acquaintance.

I suspect the validity of the new wave of research in this area just as much as I suspected the old wave. The latter was male-researcher dominated and tended to concentrate on male managers from a male perspective, which was, almost certainly unconsciously, heavily biased against female managers and their qualities. The new wave tends to be almost the gender reverse of this, and seems just as unconsciously biased in favour of the female manager.

To me, for example, the old adage about the corrupting qualities of power contains, like many such dictums, a great deal of truth which applies irrespective of the sex of the power holder.

Track records

It is too easy to dismiss the evidence of the track records of some past women managers in education as inadmissible in the present day context. We did, after all, have a long period in which single sex educational organisations at the secondary and tertiary levels meant that, no matter how disadvantaged women undoubtedly were in the general pattern of organisational management, they were leaders of institutions of considerable size and stature in what were seen as their special preserves.

Furthermore, there was a lengthy period after such institutions became co-educational when the tradition of having a woman in charge was at least some counterweight to the blatantly sexist assumption that the change in status meant that men were now the more appropriate leaders.

Many of those of us who had worked under female principals in teacher training colleges, and later the colleges of education, could recognise that the brilliant characterisation by Sheila Hancock of the role of the eponymous 'Prin' in Andrew Davies' stage play was not a figment of a warped imagination.

'Prin' was not the only one in her position with the withering sarcasm and hectoring wit to reduce her staff to snivelling wrecks. A decade and more after one female principal of my acquaintance had retired, I have seen colleagues, male and female, display nervous tics on entering a committee room long since converted from the aforementioned principal's flat. A summons to that room in the 'good old days' was the equivalent of a walk down Death Row.

Males do not have a monopoly on autocracy. I have no doubt that there are women managers who are facilitating nurturers. I have seen some of them in action. On the other hand, I do happen to have worked for male bosses who were not the bullying autocrats of the stereotypical legend but were, on the contrary, very helpful mentors and coaches as I climbed the career ladder.

I hasten to add that I have also worked for male bosses who appeared to derive their main satisfaction in life from the sadistic mishandling of subordinates. When I observe the managers of others in education, I see both males and females who possess many of the positive qualities now being extolled by the management gurus. I also see managers of both sexes who appear to be serving apprenticeships to enable them to go on to be the despotic and tyrannical rulers of some benighted fiefdom elsewhere.

In other words, I don't think it's at all helpful to give male and female labels to managerial qualities. Perhaps what we should be looking for as the ideal in conceptual but not, I hasten to add, in biological terms, is the androgynous manager who can call on the best of the so-called masculine and feminine managerial characteristics as the situation demands.

Carrots and sticks

A GROUP OF Dutch students who were training to be primary school teachers recently made a study visit to the Faculty of Education at the University of Central England in Birmingham. As part of their programme, they spent one and a half days visiting four primary school in the area.

Their written evaluation of the visit included the following comments about the school assemblies which they observed: 'Assemblies are used to impart all kinds of information and for performances, singing, Religious Instruction and for publicly rewarding the achievements or behaviour of individual pupils. This last aspect, in particular, produced very mixed feelings in a number of us. The discipline and order, but especially the fact that pupils were, in front of a large group, put in the spotlight and rewarded with a distinction, a lollipop and applause, caused more concern than just the raising of eyebrows. Our emotions made us forget how all this originated, how wonderful the feeling of togetherness can be, how good it feels to be publicly rewarded and how strongly our Calvinistic tradition has taught us that you must be rewarded in silence but publicly called to account . . . '

These comments have sparked off a number of thoughts in my mind about rewards and punishments in relation not only to the performance of school pupils in particular but also in the context of school management in general.

From school to adult life

First of all, I suspect that there is a disjunction between school and adult society in England in this respect (although I would hesitate to indulge in any speculation about these matters in the different cultural contexts of the more Celtic parts of the British Isles). Whereas we are apparently more prone to give public praise to individual pupils in schools than our Dutch colleagues, it is my experience that we do not operate in similar ways in an adult work setting. On one never-to-be-forgotten occasion, I once singled out a colleague for public praise. As his line manager, I had been very impressed with a particular achievement which had come to fruition just before the particular gathering at which I made my public pronouncement. It was borne home to me very quickly after the meeting in various ways that this had been very badly received by the rest of the group. 'If I was going to praise X for this, why hadn't I praised Y and Z for that and the other?' and so on. I learned from that episode that it was wiser to praise in private than in public in that particular work context.

Praise may be difficult for the English boss to give in general. Janet Daley, in one of her newspaper columns some time ago, argued that she had found over a more than twenty year period that bosses on this side of the Atlantic were far less likely than their American counterparts to praise or thank the people who work with them. Perhaps that's because there is some kind of unwritten rule in our adult English society that such praise is an embarrassment to all concerned. This seems to me to be a great pity if it relates to praise which is given privately rather than publicly. Such private praise need have no demotivating effects on others. Public praise, on the other hand, does have potential counter-productive elements to it in our English adult culture.

I sometimes think that some of our secondary school pupils have already latched on to this fact, which would go some way to explain the references to 'teachers' pets', 'crawlers' or 'creeps' when their classmates are on the receiving end of public praise.

I happen to be very familiar, at second hand, with the work practices of a British-based subsidiary of an American company which operates very much according to the model of the parent company in the USA. In this case, the public 'thank you' is very much a part of standard work practice. It often takes the form of a tangible reward, either in cash terms or the equivalent thereof, which is publicly announced in the firm's regular newsletter. There is, however, undoubtedly a down-side to this. Those who do not receive these public rewards are apparently being spurred on by their company to do better. One such company actually sends the details of which of their sales force have received this month's prize of an exotic holiday for the family not to the employee's work address but to their home address, so that the partner of the employee can become another agent in the 'spurring on' process.

David Mamet's stage and subsequent screen play *Glengarry Glen Ross* shows this approach to 'motivation' at its most cutthroat. Of the four competing salesmen who are the central characters, the most successful will win a Cadillac at the end of the month, the second will win a set of steak knives and the bottom two will get the sack. As a metaphor for the 'winners and losers' culture of the USA, this is perhaps the best theatrical representation since Arthur Miller's *Death of a Salesman*. I sometimes get the feeling that this is an American culture in which there is no perceived discontinuity between school and adult life.

From the comments of my Dutch colleagues, it also seems as if the Calvinist culture in the Netherlands has no discontinuity in this respect either, except that in their culture public praise and reward is acceptable neither in the school nor in the adult society. There is a downside to this, too. Indeed, one of my Dutch colleagues went on to describe this as one of the features of life in the Netherlands which she liked least, because it was linked to what she saw as a general attitude which frowned upon individuals 'getting too big for their boots' at any stage in life. This, in her view, could be an intolerant brake on individual aspirations.

Sub-cultures

These national cultural differences reflect age old tensions between the individual and society, and in each society there are sub-cultures which, in any case, buck the general trend. The point that I am trying to make is that the English in this, as in so many other respects, seem much more ambivalent about their attitudes towards competition and community, which makes for particular difficulties with certain managerial developments such as *performance-related pay*. This is already in operation in some sectors of the world of education and, whether we like it or not, it would appear to be only a matter of time under the present government before it is universally applied across the public sector in general.

What are the lessons which might be learned from my earlier remarks about its application within our national culture? First of all, I would suggest that public statements as to who have received performance-related bonuses would be very counter-productive indeed in our culture. 'If X, then why not Y?' is almost bound to be the complaint of the day and, unlike promotions, this is going to be an annually repeatable complaint on the basis of the systems at present being operated. Indeed, if annually paid performance-related bonuses become the order of the day then, at a certain time each year, each individual is going to know if he or she received a bonus, whether or not this is made public. On the evidence of my own sector of education, there is only going to be enough cash in the government-funded kitty to provide bonuses for one in four of the work force at most. The issue then is whether or not the individual who has not received a bonus this year feels motivated to strive harder to receive one the following year.

My own feeling, based partly upon the research findings of Herzberg and others, and partly on gut reaction, is that the power for demotivation for these individuals is greater than the power for motivation of others. They are, in a sense, being 'ticked off' for not doing 'outstanding' work that year. For every four workers, therefore, one is being rewarded and three are, in effect, being punished. In our culture, this is not likely to encourage the group as a whole to operate as a more motivated work team. Indeed, precisely the opposite effect is likely to occur. Why should X help Y to a better performance if this means that Y might get paid more than X as a result?

Oddly enough, this is what the guru of quality performance in the workplace, W. E. Deming, has been arguing for the last 40 years and more. The problem from our point of view now is that it was the Japanese who listened and not his own countrymen and women in the USA. It is only at a time when the Americans themselves are recognising that Japanese approaches to teamwork have resulted in better quality products that are driving their own out of the market that we in education in the UK are being forced to adopt an American model which is rapidly being discredited in its own heartland. The quality product does not appear to be easily produced in a culture which relies upon extrinsic rewards and punishments as its motivating forces.

Destroying motivation

Deming's view is that the American model has even tended to destroy the intrinsic motivation which comes from employees who enjoy their work and take a pride in what they achieve in the course of that work. Rewarding financially what is viewed by management as good performance is not very likely to produce this collective pride, particularly when, like it or not, those who are not given these extra financial rewards are going to see themselves as being financially punished even if more drastic negative sanctions are not applied against the 'losers'. This will be even more the case when the basic pay rise without bonuses is seen as derisory, which is the way most people in the public sector view their increases in recent years.

I'd like to end by quoting a paragraph from a fairly recent book on the Deming phenomenon, *Dr Deming - the Man who Taught the Japanese about Quality* by Rafael Aguayo. It seems to me to sum up admirably the basic message of this chapter: 'For any enterprise to improve, the individual within it has to be alive and well, working and living without fear, loving his *(sic)* work. What is it that destroys the individuals in corporations, schools, and government? It is the collective policies that we call modern management. Most often the reward system is the biggest individual culprit. It punishes any form of risk-taking or spontaneity. We treat our people like children or criminals or, even worse, like machines. Rather than risk failure, people in many corporations become yes-men and yes-women. They give the corporation what is rewarded ... and destroy the company, and sometimes the whole industry, in the process.'

This reads uncomfortably like the message which Mark Tully was trying to communicate to the management of the BBC in his famous lecture denouncing 'Birtism', or what he alleged was management by fear in the corporation. But Birtism is only one example of the larger issue of the application of 'Thatcherism' to the management of the public sector in general and to education in particular. One sector of education after another has been 'Thatcherised' in this way and the process continues long after Mrs Thatcher's departure from the House of Commons. Is this really the way we want our English education system to go?

Spreading the load

THIS CHAPTER was written as an unusually serious comment on an official report which was dubbed 'The Report of the Three Wise Men' by the popular press because the views of its three male authors were in line with the government thinking of the day. Maybe there is some irony in the fact that one of the Three Wise Men was Chris Woodhead, now Chief Inspector Woodhead . . .

According to the 'Three Wise Men' report, there are two broad approaches to primary headship. It argues:

'On the one hand, the emphasis is on the head as administrator; on the other, the emphasis is squarely on the need to provide educational leadership. There is a view at present in England that the introduction of LMS means that the primary head must become an administrator or chief executive. We reject this view absolutely. The task of implementing the National Curriculum and its assessment arrangements requires headteachers, more than ever, to retain and develop the role of educational leader. Primary schools exist to provide a curriculum which fosters the development of their pupils. Headteachers must take the leading role in ensuring the quality of curricular provision and they cannot do this without involving themselves directly and centrally in the planning, transaction and evaluation of the curriculum.' (Paragraph 152)

Some primary school headteachers appear to have been somewhat taken aback by this view of their role, but the issue is driven home in paragraph 162:

'The final point we wish to emphasise is that the headteacher should lead by example. They may not have timetabled teaching commitments, but all headteachers should teach. Actions speak louder than words and the headteacher's teaching can and must exemplify their vision of what the school might become.'

Now in my experience, primary heads' reaction to these comments has been that this is all well and good but how are they going to teach *and* be curriculum leaders *and* at the same time cope with the enormously expanded administrative load which has been heaped on their shoulders, by LMS in particular and the speed of educational reform in general?

This reaction only confirms the findings of some research I carried out a few years ago with primary heads, when the shape of LMS to come was beginning to emerge. It was already clear then that the 'chief executive' role of the primary head was looming ever larger. The stated perception of most of the heads whom I interviewed was that they were very reluctant at that time to abandon or even reduce their teaching and curriculum leadership roles, but that this was being forced upon them by the changing circumstances.

Stress

One head, who reckoned he was teaching just under half a full timetable, clearly indicated the kind of stress this was causing him:

'I have given it some considerable thought and the way I get over it is by doing a lot of work at night. I seriously think there is going to come a time in the near future when, for my own sanity, my own stress health, I maybe have to come to a decision that I will do less at home and more on school time, and therefore the children will suffer again ... I am now doing less teaching than I would like to do . . . I mean, as a headteacher I think I must obviously be regarded to have certain administrative and organisational abilities and qualities that allow me to run a school. But having said that, having come through, one of my prime attributes must be to teach.'

This, in many ways, typifies the reactions of the primary school heads I interviewed. They were very reluctant to lose the reality of their 'headteacher' title which, after all, does indicate the way their role had been perceived historically by the outside world. On the other hand, their attempts to maintain this reality were becoming increasingly frustrated by the weight of their other administrative duties.

It has to be admitted, though, that even then there was a significant minority among those I interviewed who almost welcomed an abandonment of teaching. This did not appear to me to be because they did not enjoy their teaching, but because they felt that their dual role of teacher/administrator was becoming impossibly burdensome as the 'administrator' part became almost all-consuming. Furthermore, once they had abandoned the teaching role, they felt in some cases that they were less well positioned to offer curricular leadership and had, therefore, delegated this role to the deputy head.

Majority shift

In recent years, in my informal experience, the majority of heads with this dual role have shifted appreciably towards such a position. The predominantly managerial nature of their changed role has become apparent to them all, and more of them have felt that, to carry out their administration at all effectively, they have had to cut down or cut out their teaching and curricular leadership roles.

From the start, this shift in emphasis has not been viewed enthusiastically by many class teachers. Writing in the NAS/UWT Journal in 1988, Gray epitomised the reaction of many class teachers:

'Over the last few years, being a headteacher has become more and more identified with the term 'management' and less and less with the profession of teaching . . . Of course there is a management side to headship, but the crux of the matter is how they see themselves, with whom do they identify, how do they wish to be known, what is at the heart of the job? Over-emphasis on management is asking to become an extension of bureaucracy ... It may seem attractive to some to wipe the chalk dust from their fingers and don the spurious status of a sub-species of management, but in reality they are distancing themselves from the profession, weakening their influence and losing the respect of the colleagues on whom they rely.'

What has now happened with the publication of the report of the 'Three Wise Men' is that this attitude has appeared to heads to be shared by 'those in authority'. This seems to have reduced some primary heads almost to despair. They can see no way in which they can perform their dual role to their own professional satisfaction, let alone anyone else's.

I sympathise with their stance on this, but I can also see the force of the arguments of the 'Three Wise Men' and of those class teachers who echo the thoughts of Gray. Managers who lose touch with the essential purposes of the organisations they manage very quickly become bad managers. Schools are ultimately organisations, the main purpose of which is to promote pupils' learning. That's the main managerial text. Everything else is sub-text or commentary on that text. Even in large secondary schools, many heads of my acquaintance do an (admittedly) very small amount of regular teaching for this very reason.

Expectation

By contrast, most primary schools are very small units as far as staff numbers are concerned. In such small units, there is an expectation on the part of most staff that they will operate as a team in which the head, as 'team leader', and certainly as curricular leader, will take an active teaching role for at least some of the time. For that to be a satisfactory teaching role, through which the head can lead by example, it requires forward planning and purposeful follow-up. If this teaching is organised on a rota basis, it can provide the head with an excellent opportunity to meet classes and to get to know individuals. It can also help the pupils themselves to identify the head as a teacher and not just as an authority figure seen at the school assembly, etc.

These conditions are *not* met by the kind of emergency cover teaching which happens when a member of staff reports ill and the head takes over the class at very short notice, a role which is relinquished as soon as the member of staff returns. Yet that is the main, or in some cases the only, teaching which some primary heads are now able to fit into their schedule.

How, then, to square the circle? The only 'solution' which seems possible to me is one in which heads retain the space for a teaching role, albeit reduced, by sharing out a substantial part of the administration amongst the staff of the school as a whole. For this kind of delegation to be possible, a considerable cultural shift needs to take place in many primary schools. It has not, up to now, been a part of the mind-set of many primary school teachers that they are not only teachers but also managers. Teaching itself, however, can be viewed as a form of managing.

The management of pupils' learning does not strike me as a bad definition of teaching. We certainly refer constantly to class 'management'. Most teachers have, in fact, considerable managerial expertise, and there is no reason why that can not be applied to general school issues. In fact, the trends in this direction are already there with the appointment of curriculum leaders etc. I am only arguing for an extension of these existing trends.

If primary school teachers want their heads to remain in touch with class teaching, and to fulfil the curricular leadership role, they will have to take on, as a *quid pro quo,* more of the growing administrative load themselves, so that space is created for it to be possible. It was, after all, one of the implications of the letter of the School Management Task Force to all teachers and governors in 1990 that all staff would need help to improve their management skills because school management had to be a collective effort.

For this process to work effectively, the extra administrative tasks delegated to class teachers will have to appear in their job descriptions and be known to their colleagues and to school governors. Only by such a public process will the organisational responsibilities be clearly allocated and due notice taken of them. Such practices have been common in most secondary schools for a very long time now, and some primary schools are also well advanced in this respect. The time has now come for all primary schools to move further in this direction.

Every second counts

JUDGING BY THE ever-increasing number of schools asking for training days on the subject of time management, it is clear that there are currently an awful lot of teachers at all levels who simply don't find there are enough hours in the day. The standard dilemma seems to be that, if they try to do their jobs to anything approaching their own satisfaction, they find they have no time left over for any other sort of life (as their families are constantly reminding them).

'Twas ever thus, responds the cynic, but I think there are grounds for concluding that in recent years the dilemma has become much more acute for many more people. So there's a strong case for attending time management courses to see what help can be offered.

However, I have a couple of residual worries when I run such courses myself. Firstly, improving your personal time management should not be seen as an alternative to, or substitute for, collective action to bring about structural changes in jobs with excessive work loads. This is rather akin to going to your boss with a work-related stress problem which you think is affecting you and your colleagues generally, and being told that you personally need to go on a stress management course. You could be right if you then conclude that it's your boss and your employers who ought to be going on the stress management course in order to understand how their policies and decisions impact on others. As the man said: 'If your fish are dying, try taking a look at your aquarium.'

Secondly, there is no one magic knack of time management which can be 'taught' on one or two day training courses as a standard formula which will improve the lot of all participants. What you *can* offer as a trainer are sets of ideas and techniques which individuals can test out for themselves to see which, if any, work for them. Nowhere in management training, in my view, is the axiom of 'different strokes for different folks' more appropriate.

There are two polarised extremes from which contributions on this topic are frequently delivered. The first is the 'superorganised' stance adopted by those who claim to have managed their time in meticulous fashion since they acquired the 'gift' of time management. The other stance, much favoured by humorists, is that of being supremely disorganised, from whose daily catastrophes much can be learned by those slightly less afflicted by chaos. Most of us actually fall between these two extremes, although there may be highs and lows when we get close to either end of the continuum.

I do not offer these thoughts from the perspective of someone who can survive on a regular regime of four hours sleep a night, as various 'superpeople' are reputed to do. Both Napoleon and Mrs Thatcher were variously reported as regarding the seven-to-eight-hours-sleep-a-night merchants as 'weaklings', so maybe these are time management thoughts for weaklings. Certainly the assumption will be that you are not going to solve your time management problems by sleeping less and simply lengthening your working day. That way lies eventual breakdown for the majority of the working population. Nor is it a solution to take even more time away from the family in order to cope with the workload.

In my view, a healthy balance between home life and work life is the target towards which we should all be aiming. The expressed desire to spend more time with one's family has become a euphemism among politicians for having just been dumped from the cabinet, but this is merely one more demonstration, as far as I am concerned, of the distorted set of values of our elected representatives.

Body clock

The first step is to look at your own body clock. Most of us are familiar with people who seem to operate more efficiently either early in the morning or late at night. The owls and the early birds both seem to have great difficulty in accepting that the rest of the world does not operate with the same body clock as their own, and woe betide any marriage between an owl and an early bird – a plea in the divorce court of basic incompatibility can be confidently expected at some point in the future. Either that, or a plea of justifiable homicide in a different court altogether.

Exceptionally, I have had members of training courses who have claimed to be at their peak of efficiency *both* late at night *and* first thing in the morning but, under intense interrogation by their grievously envious colleagues, these same individuals have usually eventually admitted to being absolutely useless (to employ a euphemistic paraphrase), as far as effective work is concerned, for a considerable period in the middle of the day. This pattern is, of course, built into some whole cultures – usually, but not exclusively, where the midday heat is held to legitimise the siesta or the very, very long lunch.

The key point is to understand how your own body clock seems to have been set, either by the great watchmaker in the sky, or by selective evolution (for those who prefer the rather more prosaic Darwinian hypothesis), and to operate your time management accordingly.

To illustrate the point from personal experience, I always wake early, and usually, but unfortunately not invariably, brightly. As a teenager I tended, for various reasons, to arrive at school well before most of my fellow pupils, and I discovered that the homework I did on arrival at school, on the mornings when I *was* bright eyed and bushy tailed, was often that which achieved my better marks. In later life, I have capitalised on this by being regularly at my desk at least an hour before the start of the scheduled work day, which means that an 'early' start can be two hours before the agreed 'kick-off' time.

Starting in this way for a night owl could be very stressful, but for me it's a way of avoiding stress (time management and stress management are inextricably linked. Time management is really a synonym for gaining more control over your life). I'm at work before the traffic jams; I can do productive and creative work at this hour; and there's none of that last-minute rush to line up the work for the day as the kick-off time approaches. I usually also benefit from listening to audio cassette tapes (for brushing up my French or German, for example) in the car on the journey to work.

However, I am making no individual claim to exceptional capabilities on this account. While not falling personally into the 'up before seven, dead before eleven' category, I have observed that other colleagues can continue working effectively at their desks long after five o'clock in the afternoon, a time when I am no longer capable of the sustained concentration required for that kind of work. At that point I need a significant break, preferably at home. I also never, under any circumstances, listen to 'educational' tapes during the car journey home, when the effort involved for me would be phenomenal.

It would be a disaster for me to work in that kind of office culture, reportedly common in Japan, where even the most junior manager would not think it proper to leave his or her desk before the usually workaholic top manager quits the office late at night. I can cope with meetings and teaching sessions in what for me are the twilight hours, because the stimulus provided by the interaction with students and staff keeps the adrenalin flowing, but any concentrated desk work I do after five is frankly likely to be of inferior quality. So the trick is to recognise this and to organise work accordingly. My best time to do the most demanding paper work of the day is, without a shadow of a doubt, the early morning. Reading the daily newspaper, on the other hand (or 'scanning the environment', to use management-speak), is something I do for relaxation, so that's best reserved for the evening in my case. With others, the reverse could easily be the case.

Analysing work patterns

To analyse your work patterns each day for a set period, the best way is through some form of log. There are various ways of doing this, and a good detailed description of the different possibilities is contained in 'Using time efficiently' by I Craig (in *Primary School Management In Action*, I Craig (ed) 1987, Longman). Such a time log, when completed, can be a very revealing picture of the kinds of activities to which you are devoting most of your time. You would not be the first manager to discover that, amongst these activities, the trivial many are crowding out the vital few. Most managers in a wide range of occupations usually find through this kind of analysis, if they didn't already know it, that their working day all too often consists of a hectic series of brief encounters of the distinctly unromantic kind, with few periods of relative calm when any one issue can be pursued at length and in detail. Heads and deputies are no exceptions, judging from the published research.

Some researchers have even advanced the idea that far too many managers are *addicted* to 'interruptions'. These managers may actually enjoy the bursts of adrenalin that the interruptions bring with them and they provide a ready excuse, either consciously or subconsciously, for not having settled down to produce, for example, that dratted report which requires a period of intense concentration. Viewed in this light, enjoyment of interruptions may only be a form of procrastination – a way of putting off the evil day when some unpleasant nettle or other has to be grasped.

For these managers, work such as report writing, which requires their undivided attention, is often precisely the kind that they find most difficult and from which they derive least job satisfaction. 'Paper pushing' isn't half as exciting for these managers as solving other people's crises for them, even if most of these people should be coming up with solutions to their own problems.

Such managers may even welcome this upward delegation to them by their subordinates. They would almost certainly subscribe to the view of management which says 'my door is always open'.

On the contrary, I would argue, on the basis of experience, that there must be times when the door to your office isn't even slightly ajar, so that particular problems can be tackled without interruption. Certainly the more conventional direction, of downward delegation of tasks to the appropriate level, is essential if heads and senior management in schools are going to control their own use of time effectively and focus on the goals at which they have consciously decided they and the school need to aim.

Keys

One of the keys to effective time management is deciding which issues demand serious and lengthy consideration, which can be dealt with lightly and quickly, and which should be passed on to others or even ignored. The old maxim that you shouldn't let the urgent issues drive out the important ones is very relevant in this context. In other words, some system of prioritisation is essential.

It is precisely the value of this process of prioritisation and goal setting which, in my own experience, the courses in this field conducted by Time Manager International (TMI) drive home best. This organisation, founded by the Dane Claus Moller in 1975, now employs over 500 people in 35 countries. Its annual turnover of $100 million is some testimony to the demand from managers in all fields for help with this aspect of their work. Even if you don't find in the long term that the personal organiser which goes with the standard two day course is really as helpful as you had hoped (my own lame excuse being that my secretary could never get the hang of how to tie it into the conventional diary system which she was determined to maintain), the lessons it teaches about linking your daily, weekly and monthly tasks to your long term goals are invaluable. The basic argument is that without objectives, you don't know what to do; without priorities, you don't know what to do first; and without deadlines, you don't know when to do anything.

Certainly my 'to do' list is now an organised system along the principles inculcated on the TMI course, whereas beforehand it was a seemingly ever-expanding rag-bag of uncoordinated scraps of paper. That very unstructured approach gave me no sense of priorities or of control over the work load ahead. Now I use a thought processing system *(PC-Outline)* on my personal computer, which allows me to organise and reorganise my tasks according to the TMI gospel on a fairly continuous basis and in a speedy and painless fashion.

It still doesn't mean, however, that my desk is the totally uncluttered model currently regarded as so desirable in management circles; for one thing, the 3M 'Post-it' stickers are just too tempting an invitation for me to decorate the spaces around my in-tray with what I see as the really urgent tasks of the moment. But at least, these days, I can welcome visitors without resembling one of those bartenders in the cowboy films of my youth. Those were the characters whose hands alone were just visible above the bar, sliding the drinks along while the gunfights took place! At least the clutter never reaches those former mountainous heights on my desk nowadays, and maybe that in itself is some tribute to the lessons that time management courses can teach.

Testing your wits

READERS WILL BE familiar with those ubiquitous case studies of managerial dilemmas which participants on management training courses are asked to 'resolve'. Somehow, they never seem to match up to the full lunatic complexity of managerial life in the real world. I well remember returning from one such week-long course where we had been faced at one point by an 'in-tray exercise' with some twenty items on which to make our considered judgement in one hour from a standing start.

The actual in-tray which awaited me on the Monday morning back at the ranch made the course exercise seem like child's play by comparison. Members of staff appeared to have done little in the previous week except pursue vendettas, destroy or lose vital equipment, harass colleagues and students, etc. Alternatively, they had spent the week doing none of these but had actually been writing fictitious memos of fiendish ingenuity to each other (copy to yours truly), which were designed to give me an instant nervous breakdown on my return.

The prime motive for this would obviously be so that one of them could take on my apparently cushy number which allowed me to swan off to desirable conference locations for a week at a time while they slaved in the galleys to preserve my life of Riley. I tended towards the latter hypothesis because my master strategy in dealing with this in-tray load was to ignore most of it as soon as I had read through the contents, and instead to sit back and wait for the after-shocks. As the various crises threatened by the in-tray memos consistently failed to re-materialise in the weeks which followed, I concluded that masterly inactivity had once again proved its worth. Who says you learn nothing on management courses?

In point of fact, I have a colleague who has clearly been to more advanced courses than mine because she claims that she bins such awkward-looking in-trays *before* she reads the contents. It's through this sort of attention to detail that you can hone your time-management skills to ever sharper levels of effectiveness.

I can now offer headteachers and others the following in-tray exercises which are carefully designed to give a greater match to the daily reality of life in schools:

An inspector calls

It is the last school day before the end of the Autumn Term. You are aware that sometime towards the end of next term your school is due for an OFSTED inspection. Your mind is already running ahead beyond Christmas and the New Year to all the rehearsal lessons that will have to be run next term, the posters of exotic European locations which will have been brought in to liven up the walls of the modern languages rooms, the live animals to be purchased for the pets' corner, the policy statements which will have to be fabricated in every sense of the word, etc. As you idly daydream along these lines, there is a knock at the door and your friendly neighbourhood Registered Inspector arrives unexpectedly 'to make some preliminary arrangements for next term'.

You spend the next hour desperately trying to pull the wool over her eyes. You praise the wit and wisdom of Chris Woodhead and Nick Tate, and your nose shows no tendency to develop Pinocchio-type characteristics; you extol the virtues of whole class teaching in serried ranks and rows and there is no sound of any cock crow; you refer to the splendid effect that your new system of interviews of parents applying to enrol their offspring is having on the quality of your pupil intake, and no clinking of pieces of silver can be heard.

At the end of the hour, you are congratulating yourself on having lived on your wits just one more time and you insist on accompanying the inspector to her car. You are somewhat dismayed to be told that her Volvo is in the far car park as this means you are going to have to walk the length of the main corridor to get there.

All is quiet on the Western Front, however, until you reach the last classroom in the corridor. It is unfortunately impossible to ignore the hullabaloo coming from inside the room, so you put on your best responsible headteacher/troubleshooter frown and open the door. Miss Jenkinson is sitting tied to her chair at the front of the class, bound and gagged. Pupils are dancing around her, whooping and hollering as loudly as possible.

a) Which aspect of the National Curriculum do you claim Miss Jenkinson is delivering?
b) What views do you claim to hold on 'creative projects'?
c) Discuss the pros and cons of taking the gag out of Miss Jenkinson's mouth.

Sex, drugs, and rock 'n' roll

It is Monday morning. Before you even leave home, you receive a telephone call from a very croaky Mark Jones, one of the younger members of staff, to the effect that he is obviously in the early stages of laryngitis and will have to stay in bed for the day. He has no lesson plans he can provide because he has been in bed most of the weekend and it is a minor miracle that he has been able to crawl to the phone. He is not at all certain he will make it all the way back to the bed. He is sure, however, that his colleagues will understand his predicament and will rally round to cover his teaching in his absence.

You arrive at school and organise the cover list. As this is pinned up on the staff notice board, you observe Angela Fortescue go very pale and slump into a chair at the realisation that she is down to take the last two periods of Mark Jones's day, which consist of moral education for the school leavers' class. You ignore this, along with the muttered expletives and obscenities from others who are also on the hit list.

Later that morning, you receive a plain brown envelope in your pigeon-hole. Inside you find the following message made up of letters cut out of newspapers and pasted on to card (you note in passing that this is not the kind of newsprint favoured by the broadsheet press).

'It's about time you realised what that cunning sod Mark Jones is up to. He does regular gigs with "Harzwolf" for which he plays lead guitar. He refers to his work with us as "the day job". This is increasingly inaccurate as we haven't been seeing too much of him during the day these past few months, have we? Were you aware he was given a formal caution by the police for possession of amphetamines after the Glastonbury do? If you aren't, we don't know why, as he's been boasting about it to his pupils ever since.

'Which brings us on to Mary Morris in the lower sixth. Are we still supposed to be *in loco parentis* these days or are we just loco? Who do you think gave her that nose stud she's been sporting this past fortnight? Isn't it about time you started to earn that ridiculous salary you get for pushing pieces of paper around?

'The Well-wishers'

Just as you finish reading this, your secretary buzzes you to the effect that the parents of Mary Morris are outside your office, desperate to speak to you as they haven't seen Mary since she left home to go to a gig on Saturday night. She was supposed to be staying over with a friend that night but had been expected back on Sunday evening. They have telephoned the parents of the friend who say they haven't seen Mary in weeks. Your secretary also adds the reassuring news that Mary has not turned up for school this morning.

What is your next move, and your overall strategy, bearing in mind that Mark Jones is also the only son of your chair of governors? The latter happens to be a lawyer by profession and regards Mark as a potential creative genius . . .

Taking the heat

It is early afternoon on a particularly hot summer's day. You have been managing by walking about the playing fields with the LEA groundsman, Jim Spenser, who has your school to attend to amongst very many others. You never miss the opportunity to chat to him as:

(a) it gets you out into the open air and, more importantly,
(b) he is a mine of information about the other schools in
    the area.

You are returning to your office, chortling at his gossipy anecdotes about the latest antics of some of your more maverick headteacher colleagues, when you observe Wayne Andrews (or the 'poison dwarf', as he is known to your staff) standing outside your door. You assume he has been sent there by a teacher and you wonder what new trouble he is into this time.

To your surprise, you learn that for once he is here of his own accord. He has come to register a complaint against Harry Jones, one of the older members of staff, who he alleges punched him in the face during the lunch break. He points somewhat unnecessarily to an ugly red bruise on the side of his face which you can immediately see will come out very fetchingly in the colour photos so beloved of lawyers and journalists.

You take a deep breath and enquire how this unfortunate *contretemps* came to take place. Wayne's version is that a group of his mates had been calling out Harry Jones' particularly unfortunate nickname behind the latter's back as was oft their wont on hot summer's days when their blood was up (you realise that you are mentally transcribing this dialogue into pseudo-Elizabethan either as a tribute to the groundsman's poetic namesake or as an escapist flight of fancy, or both). Mr Jones had allegedly rounded on them and seized Wayne, 'as he's got it in for me'.

Wayne had been roughly pushed against the wall, and, as any upstanding youth determined to save face would, he had pushed back. Inexplicably, as far as Wayne was concerned, this had

79

apparently enraged Mr Jones, who had then punched him in full view of his friends. What are you going to do about it?

What *are* you going to do about it, taking the following considerations into account?

a) Harry Jones and his staff room clique have been a thorn in your flesh ever since you took up this headship. You think he thoroughly deserves his unfortunate nickname (which you will have gathered, by now, is not publishable in a book of this nature). You know he regards you as a wet wimp whose woolly liberalism has led to a disastrous decline in the school's discipline since the days of your predecessor, 'Slasher' Grant. This might be just the chance you have been looking for to ease Harry into premature retirement, under threat of more draconian measures if he decides to resist. On the other hand, what will be your standing with the staff if Harry is able to call your bluff and make you back down . . . ?

b) Wayne and his mates (and even more so, their parents) are very familiar with the procedures of the law and any chances of payment for damages will have them heading for the courts and the media a lot faster than you can say 'society of greed'. You can seriously do without this, given the existing situation of falling rolls. Headlines about 'heavy handed Harry' may actually *encourage* a few parents of the 'spare the rod variety' but it will put off a good deal more.
How do you convince Wayne that it is in his own interests to tell his parents the bruise was the result of a fight with his mates? How are you going to convince his mates to go along with this? How are you going to achieve all this and still have the threat of bringing in the law to hold over Harry?

c) Spenser, the groundsman, is still on the school premises and there is very little which escapes his beady vulture's eye. Whatever the outcome, it will be around all the other schools in the neighbourhood in no time.

You have 15 minutes to write down your answers to this conundrum. Do not write on both sides of the paper at the same time. If you come up with a good solution, I know you will have at least one local head of my acquaintance deeply interested.

On bossing secretaries about
(For male headteachers only!)

NEVER APPOINT male secretaries. They are far more likely to get uppity. What you need is a wife substitute. Always remember she's at your constant beck and call. If she claims she has other pressures, give her a talking-to about prioritisation. That means you first and the rest nowhere.

Similarly, the last thing she needs is a job description. This just provides opportunities for the barrackroom lawyers to claim that some things are not their responsibility. Everything you ask her to do is, by definition, her responsibility. If you are forced by interfering bureaucrats to give her a job description, make it as brief and as vague as possible and end with the words: 'In addition, she must carry out the reasonable instructions of the headteacher.' By definition, all of your instructions are reasonable.

You can't as yet prevent her from joining a trades union, but you can certainly actively discourage the notion. Her isolation from any possibility of group solidarity is one of your strongest power levers. On the other hand, if she insists on allying herself with the school cleaners, that's her funeral.

Make the assumption that she is well below you in intelligence or any other pecking order that's going (this is precisely why the word 'underling' was invented in the first place).

Always dictate letters or write them out in longhand first. Never allow her to draft letters for you. That would be tantamount to admitting she is just as capable as you in this respect.

Never make a phone call when she could take a memo from you on the subject. Memos are tangible proofs of the need for your existence and reminders to all and sundry who get copies that you're the boss around this place. (This is known in the trade as reinforcing the power differential.) Never trust her to send a letter or memo out without your checking them first. If ever you do find an error, then criticise her, preferably in front of others. That should keep her on her toes. There's nothing wrong with your being a perfectionist in these matters.

She doesn't even have to make mistakes to get the rough end of your temper. If you've been having a bad time at home, you've got to take it out on someone, and who's better positioned for this than your secretary? Capriciously punitive behaviour on your part should make her hyper-attentive to your every whim. Treat 'em mean and keep 'em keen!

Inferior

Teaching staff may have vague ideas about being colleagues, but such fanciful notions certainly don't apply in her case. Encourage teaching staff to see her as their inferior. They'll soon pick this up from the way they see you belittle her. At the same time, also encourage teaching staff to go to her as the first port of call with any general queries about the management of the school. She should be expected to be a walking encyclopaedia as regards staff handbook queries. Certainly you and the teachers haven't got the time to read it.

Don't see her as entitled to any share of the staff development budget. Develop into precisely what, in her case? The very notion might give her ideas above her station. She certainly doesn't need new skills for a routine job like hers.

If you can't find something in the filing system, immediately assume she has lost it. Misfiling equals losing as far as you are

concerned, anyway. This is precisely why you don't give her total
responsibility for organising filing and information systems. If
it's something important, file it yourself. That way, you'll know
where to look next time the issue crops up. Mind you, if you
can't then remember whether you filed it or not, or, if you did,
where you filed it, then you can always go back to your first
assumption.

'No task is too demeaning for your secretary. She doesn't know
the meaning of the word. She is overjoyed to buy the birthday
cards for your nearest and dearest which it's her job to remind
you to send. Sewing on buttons for you is an unalloyed pleasure
for her. As for keeping you supplied with regular cups of coffee,

she wouldn't know what to do with herself if that responsibility were taken away from her.

Don't bother to plan your diary with her each day. It all adds to the unexpected variety in her day when staff arrive claiming prior appointments she's unaware of. You don't mind if staff turn up without appointments anyway. The day would be very boring if you didn't have staff dropping in for a chat. Whenever you give her a job to do, keep hovering over her shoulder to see how she's getting on with it. Don't hesitate to point out that she's not doing it the way you wanted, even though you hadn't given precise instructions to start with. It's only when you see what she's doing that you realise what you really wanted in the first place anyway.

There's no reason why she shouldn't be working on three jobs simultaneously. Your mind keeps flitting from one to the other and coming up with new ideas on all three fronts, so she'll just have to accommodate to your work practices. Show her who's in control. Unpredictability is all part of your creative charm.

If she comes up with a really good idea for improving the system, implement it but make sure you claim all the credit. (This is, of course, an unlikely eventuality, because you never consult her about possible solutions to problems that she might be able to see better than you can. Perish the thought!)

On the other hand, if any disasters occur, put it all down to her incompetence. Remember that the main function of secretaries is to carry the can if any of your management goes noticeably awry. Don't hesitate to dictate memos which begin: 'Due to an oversight by my secretary . . .'

Delegating dirty jobs

Don't hesitate to ask her to lie on your behalf if you've gone for a round of golf. How to be economical with the truth is one of the key things she has to learn in this job. She should be grateful to you for providing her with so many opportunities to hone her skills in this respect.

Whenever you pull a fast one on others, don't just let her see you doing it, brag about it. Demonstrate what a deviously cunning brain you've got when it comes to inter-personal relationships.

This will only impress her all the more; she hasn't the intelligence herself to see what the implications are for the way you deal with her.

Don't hesitate to break promises or dishonour previous commitments if something better comes along. Get your secretary to do the dirty work of telephoning those people whom you are letting down. Tell her to feed them any old cock and bull story to placate them. She's got to learn that your diary is an ongoing narrative of creative fiction and not a series of promises to keep.

If your secretary is contacted by someone you don't want to see under any circumstances, feel free to tell her exactly what you think about the individual concerned. Badmouthing people *in absentia* is excellent therapy, and you know that your secretary will translate your profanities into some obsequiously diplomatic version of the cold shoulder. Why should she need therapy?

If there's a really big job on, such as the preparation of a report for an outside deadline, keep reminding her that the days are ticking by. That's just the extra pressure she needs to produce a good job. She should know by now that you've no faith in her ability to come up with the goods without your breathing down her neck all the time.

Otherwise, don't give her complete tasks to complete but just small sections at a time, so you can keep an eye on her progress or lack of it. Never outline the whole problem to her or actually ask her how she would like to handle it. All this will help to make her realise how dependent she is upon you. It's your job to tell her what to do, not to consult her on how she sees the situation. The very idea . . . !

Deal with crises as they occur rather than wasting your time trying to plan ahead. She won't mind staying late to cope with today's damage limitation exercise.

If she should dare to suggest that her job is lacking in scope for autonomy or creativity, tell her that if she thinks *her* job's boring and frustrating, she should try *yours*.

Only the echoes of my mind

'Ev'rybody's talkin at me
I don't hear a word they're sayin'
Only the echoes of my mind.'

From the song 'Everybody's Talkin'. Words and music by Fred Neil. Published by Coconut Grove Music 1967, 1968.

ONE OF THE KEY roles of headteachers is to listen to staff who want to bring all manner of concerns from the professional to the very private to their attention. In the training manual for the headteachers from hell, this topic gets a section all of its own which goes as follows:

Always instruct your secretary to agree to fix meetings in your diary only when the member of staff initiating the meeting is absolutely explicit as to what the purpose of the meeting is. Your secretary must also remember that you are, by definition, already booked up for a fortnight.

Make it quite clear from the moment they come in that you see this as an unwelcome interruption of the vastly overcrowded schedule that you are condemned to work to on their account. You don't need to say a word to convey this. Where you sit, how you sit, or even *if* you sit, will be quite enough to get your message across.

Staff very rarely have the chance to meet you on a one-to-one basis, so don't deprive them of a glimpse of your virtuoso talents as a conversationalist. There's nearly always an opportunity early on in their introduction to recall a similar problem with which you were faced earlier in your career. There's nothing they would like better than a trip down your memory lane. After all, it was the way you triumphed over similar early adversities which has brought you to where you are today, and they'd all like to end up behind a desk as big as yours, so give them the benefit of your experience . . . at length.

You will often find that the emotional charge behind some of the problems they bring to you tends to make them tongue-tied and relatively inarticulate. Help them over these potentially embarrassing moments by supplying them with the words for which they're struggling, or finish their sentences for them. They'll be ever so grateful, and are bound to admire your verbal dexterity.

Some of the staff will also have dreadfully irritating verbal quirks. Don't hesitate to give non-verbal feedback to the effect that such mannerisms drive you up the wall. How otherwise are they ever going to become aware of and get rid of these speech defects? You certainly shouldn't try to hide your own emotions in these situations. If you feel irritated or angry by some of the rubbish they're prattling, why shouldn't you show it? This way, you certainly won't get a reputation as an android calculating machine.

Verbal diarrhoea

Some staff can be appallingly long-winded and can sometimes take ages to get to the point, which just underlines the point that you know well in advance which staff to take seriously. Facilitate their delivery by summarising early on what you take their essential point to be (that's a statement, of course, and not a question. Try to avoid questions but, if they are absolutely essential, then do remember there's no question like a closed question for getting precisely the kind of response that you require). Don't hesitate to interrupt their stream of consciousness with a well-timed interjection which gets straight to the nub of the matter. You may have to talk over their own flow of verbal diarrhoea to get a word in edgeways; some of them are remarkably insensitive to your signals that you want them to shut up for the time being.

When they're talking, ignore their body language and the

emotions they may appear to be (inadequately) bottling up. You're trying to listen to words, not feelings. These feelings only get in the way of your understanding of the words they're actually uttering. You've got to make them stay on an objective plane in these kind of meetings, otherwise you'll never be able to make a logical analysis of their problems and come up with the definitive solutions.

There's also an off-chance that the whole session might deteriorate into one of those appalling occasions where what they are looking for is so-called 'genuine counselling' rather than being told what they ought to do in the circumstances. You've neither the time nor the inclination to play games of the 'in the psychiatrist's chair' kind. Anthony Clare gets paid a lot more than you for those silly parlour games he goes in for. Anyway, you much prefer Desert Island Discs with that charming Sue Lawley.

In any case, you've read quite enough about Freud, Jung and the rest to know that your own brand of amateur psycho-analysis is just as good as that of all the rest of the amateurs. All you need is a few of the tell-tale words or phrases that staff often come out with on occasions like this, and you're quite capable of making a snappy realistic diagnosis. How many times have you had to point out to them that what they're bringing to you is only the *presenting* issue? *You* know what the real underlying issues are. It's your job, after all, to have your finger on the whole school pulse and to know what the real concerns of the staff are at any given time. They're usually very grateful that you've revealed to them what it is that's really bothering them.

This also cuts out any need for all that 'reflecting back' nonsense. You don't need to check out from time to time that you're understanding their main ideas by giving tentative feedback on what you think they're trying to convey. You know full well what they are saying, and what a fine lot of off-the-point waffle it so often is. All that codswallop about 'empathic listening' is typical of the kind of ivory tower academic writing that has no place in the busy real world in which you live. Have you ever heard anything as daft as the advice to 'listen with your eyes'? You might as well advise people to play the piano with their toes. And what about that all that rubbish to the effect that they should be helped to find their own solutions? If they had solutions to their problems they wouldn't be coming to you in the first place. Finding solutions to their problems for them is precisely what you're paid for.

Glazing over

Watch out for their eyes glazing over when you launch into one of your favourite themes on occasions such as these. That's a sure sign that they do not share your commitment to the school's mission, besides being highly discourteous to someone in your position of authority. Your own interventions are, of course, not open to question or interruption.

Don't bother to block off telephone calls on these occasions. They can often be a welcome distraction, particularly if the member of staff looks like launching into one of those soul-searching monologues. Why should you wish to know that they're going through identity crises? That's no excuse whatsoever for any falling away in teaching performance.

Indeed, have an arrangement with your secretary that she puts through a call of her own at prearranged intervals. Have a code worked out between you so that a key word from you means she should knock on the door in five minutes to warn you that the chair of governors is unexpectedly about to descend on the school at any moment, which means you are reluctantly forced to bring the interview to a conclusion. *Your* conclusion, that is. This a far more advanced technique than the basic 'looking regularly at your watch' type of responses. It's amazing how some people will remain oblivious even to the most obvious signals that their time is up.

On those tricky occasions where you discover too late that there's a hidden agenda to the meeting and one that might just cause some future difficulties for you, don't hesitate to whip out the old memo pad and pencil. As soon as you start taking detailed notes they'll know they've been rumbled. You're perfectly capable of listening to the rest of their spiel while writing up what you think the danger signs are. Forget all that rot about intermittent eye contact and the like. That's not to say there's not a place for the long cold stare and the impassive poker face on occasion. With some of them, that's quite a good way of breaking their flow. But essentially, you're attending to what you want to attend to. If the worst comes to the worst, break off the interview to ring through to your secretary and ask her to come in and take a shorthand account of what is being said. That usually cramps their style no end.

You'll often find, after one of your stiletto-like thrusts to the very heart of the matter, that they can be at a loss for words. Don't bask in their admiration at your lightning-fast mental agility, use the time you've saved to bring up some other issues.

You've probably been wanting to catch a word with them for ages, but your hectic schedule has crowded out any opportunity. So now's your chance to bring up those grapevine whispers of criticism of their teaching that you've picked up. It's never the wrong time for them to reflect on their mistakes and have the benefit of your vast experience on how they might improve. Again, a few anecdotes about the mistakes you made in your youth will demonstrate to them your acute self-awareness that your present level of apparently effortless expertise didn't come as easily as it might seem. That kind of modesty on your part will only make you seem all the more human to them.

Rules to make you spit!

THERE IS A sequence very early on in the film *The Caine Mutiny* which warrants careful scrutiny by all managers. The captain of the good ship Caine of the US Navy is being transferred to another command, much to the joy of the new young ship's officer, who has already quickly summed him up as a slipshod individual lacking real leadership qualities.

The ship's crew has clubbed together to buy the captain a wristwatch as a leaving present. Two crew members give him the present as he prepares to leave the ship. He immediately remonstrates with them to the effect that they ought to be perfectly well aware that it is against US Navy regulations for a ship's captain to receive presents from the crew under any circumstances. He then tells the two crestfallen deckhands to place the watch on the ship's rail next to the gangplank down which he is about to descend for presumably the last time.

As he approaches the gangplank, however, his eyes inadvertently alight on the watch, which he proceeds to pick up, loudly proclaiming to the crew that this is his lucky day as he has just 'found' a watch – which was exactly what he'd wanted for some time. The eyes of the two deckhands in particular light up in appreciation of this wily ruse which gets around the regulations without technically breaking them.

The whole point of the incident is to highlight the fact that there is a good deal more to this old sea-dog's leadership than first meets the eye. This is in stark contrast to his successor (memorably played by Humphrey Bogart), who bangs on a good deal about leadership but turns out to be a paranoid stickler for the rules whose hidebound insecurity and cowardice drive the crew ultimately to mutiny.

The general managerial lesson for all of us is that there are times when it is essential to know how to 'bend' the rules if anything worthwhile is to be achieved. After all, the quickest way for employees to wreck any organisation is to 'work to rule'. In European literature, *The Good Soldier Schweyk* is a wonderfully Czech perspective on how to subvert the army of the Austro-Hungarian Empire by obeying the letter rather than the spirit of the law during the First World War (the *Gunner Asch* stories of H.H. Kirst are the equivalent for the German Army in the Second World War).

The British Army has also not been immune to this approach in the past, and the fact that someone can be charged with 'malicious obedience' suggests that the potential for disruption by the rule book has at least been acknowledged. There is even a British Army description of someone who operates in this way which has become part of the general linguistic currency of the realm as 'the barrackroom lawyer'.

Schindler's ruse

The opposite to this style of behaviour is well manifested by the accounts of the actions of Oskar Schindler, now made famous by Keneally's book and Spielberg's film. His bending of the rules made him the archetypal 'fixer' at all levels from the Nazi hierarchy to the Jewish prisoners working in his factories. A good example of his methods of alleviating the suffering of the latter by subverting the 'rules' was his practice of 'forgetting' he had left his packet of cigarettes on a workbench. In a situation where four cigarettes could buy a loaf of bread, it is not too much to say that such 'forgetfulness' was literally life-saving. It could also, of course, help to forestall any accusation of his breaking the regulations about aiding and abetting Jewish prisoners at a time when such rulebreaking could lead to a death sentence.

My own theory as to why working to rule can be so disruptive, even in situations where rules were originally drawn up for the best of intentions, is that rule books are always being added to, but rarely does anyone ever get round to scrapping rules that are long past their sell by date. (I am reminded of the Henry Root letter to the Queen pointing out that she was always opening new buildings, etc. when it might be a greater service to the nation if she put her regal authority behind the closure of organisations which have outlived their usefulness.) Consequently, rule books grow ever fatter, to take them long past the point where anyone of good will would deign to read them.

The sixth man

There is a good example of this tendency to hang on to outdated rules and regulations in Anthony Jay's book *Management and Machiavelli*. He relates the story of how, during one Royal Artillery exercise in the 1950s on Salisbury Plain, there was a demonstration of light artillery drill. Some visiting European observers were asked for their opinions on this. Most of them confessed to being very impressed, but one of the visitors asked what the role of the sixth man in the gun crew was.

It took his colleagues in the British Army a moment or so even to recognise what he was talking about, but it quickly dawned on them that, indeed, all the work had been done by five of the six man crew. Nevertheless, their response was to the effect that this sort of exercise was always carried out by a six man crew. The observer explained that he also could count, but the sixth man had simply stood to attention throughout. The Brits – somewhat wearily, no doubt – argued that this was, indeed, the role of the sixth man.

The continental inquisitor was not going to give up so easily, so he asked why they didn't make do with five men in that case.

Nobody knew the answer. It was only much later, and after some considerable research into army archives, that the answer was discovered. The job of the sixth man was to hold the reins of the horses attached to the gun crew. The fact that the use of horses in the army had long since gone out of fashion had rather gone unnoticed as far as this rule was concerned. There's a lesson here, I think, for all those who doubt the value of outside consultants. It sometimes takes a critical stranger to query what all the insiders have taken for granted for far too long.

Rules are, in any case, often drawn up not to inform the workforce and help the manager manage but to cover the manager's back if anything of a dodgy nature should occur.

Paternosters

A good example of this occurred at one of my places of work, when one of the employees slipped and fell when trying to mount one of those perpetually moving paternoster lifts which always seemed to me to be potential death traps for anyone less than nimble on his or her pins. While completing the elaborate accident form which was a statutory requirement in such circumstances, the employee threatened to sue the company for injury.

After a while, the reply of the management arrived, referring to the fact that the account of the accident mentioned that the employee was carrying a briefcase, raincoat and umbrella when attempting to enter the paternoster (this was, in my view, an honest attempt on the employee's part to explain his apparent clumsiness in stumbling, having just run into the building to avoid a heavy shower). Quoting rule 23b of the Health and Safety Manual along the lines of 'Paternosters – Safety Regulations', the management threatened to counter-sue for negligence if a legal action were to be initiated, on the grounds that the aforementioned regulation strictly prohibited the carrying of objects when using the paternoster.

This was effective in that it removed the threat of legal action by a somewhat nervous employee noted for his general desire to live as peaceful a life as possible, but the absurdity of the rule was clear for all to see. The only effective direct counter-action on the part of the employees would have been a complete boycott of the paternosters, which would have very soon clogged up the stairs in an eleven storey building.

Displaced disgruntlement

What really happens in situations such as this is not that employees start walking up and down eleven flights of stairs humping goods, but that they displace their particular disgruntlement into other areas where protest can be registered at much less personal cost in terms of time and effort and potential sanction. The levels of displacement ingenuity in such circumstances have to be seen to be believed. Certainly, those who impose such rules and regulations may score some short term gains, but there is usually a very high longer term price to pay in terms of employee demotivation.

The golden rule about rules ought to be to have as few as possible and to make these of the 'general principle' nature, which all can see as being sensible and conducive to civilised inter-personal relations. They should be as flexible and non-constraining as possible, allowing employees to use their ingenuity in constructive rather than rule-defeating destructive ways (the real golden rule is, of course, that 'they who have the gold, rule').

Imposing regulations which employees see as outdated and/or nonsensical produces reactions which are either of the 'cowed submission' or the 'devious sabotage' variety. In neither case are these the sort of reactions which are likely to be at all productive from the organisational perspective. Ideally, you should encourage those at the sharp end to draw up their own codes of conduct. They are the ones who know which rules make sense.

To end on a more light-hearted note, there is an excellent limerick which epitomises for me the counter-productive effect of many rules and the lengths to which people will go to subvert them. It goes as follows:

There was a young man from Darjeeling
Who travelled from London to Ealing
The sign on the door
Said 'don't spit on the floor'
So he carefully spat on the ceiling.

Saved from the shredder

THE SELECTION procedure for accepting reviews of books and other products for publication is such a rigorous process that, often, editors have to reject some splendid contributions for such trivial reasons as their abject terror in the face of the draconian libel laws of this realm. Nevertheless, it seems a shame that the public does not at least gain a flavour of some of these 'rejects'. The reviews which follow were all rescued from the shredder after being rejected on such grounds as sanctimonious stupidity, sycophancy, sarcasm and subversion. All titles and authors' names have, of course, been replaced by fictitious inventions in order to protect the guilty.

Beating Deprivation: a workpack for teachers

Author: Judy Taylor
Published by Panacea Publications, Tunbridge Wells

This workpack comprises a book for pupils, teachers' notes and a video. Produced in an attractive format which allows unlimited photocopying, the written material is apparently designed to 'teach strategies whereby individuals can tackle deprivation on its own terms and defeat it'. Although there has been some academic nit-picking about its precise meaning, this is a message that has been loudly and publicly applauded by government ministers, whose praises are recorded on the back cover of the main workbook. A good example is the comment of Sir Gervaise Latimer: 'This pack gives the lie to all those who are only too ready to lay the blame for deprivation at the door of governments. If ever there was a do-it-yourself kit for pulling yourself up by your own bootstraps, this is it.'

Other commentators have placed more emphasis on the teacher's vital role in the process, stressing that if teachers were less concerned about their own pay and conditions and were instead more concerned for their pupils' welfare, we would not have so many cases of child neglect in our morning newspapers.

This reviewer particularly liked the poignant little vignettes, scattered throughout the workbook, of the lives of the great and the good who have risen to national and international prominence from very humble beginnings (although there will, unfortunately, have to be some revisions to the list of those chosen when a second edition is produced. Perhaps the next edition could be published in detachable ring binder format which would allow teachers to take prompter action to reflect the ever more rapidly changing face of society?). The young of any age need these worthy role models as heroes and heroines to look up to, as they face the challenges which lie ahead of them on the upward climb of life.

The video is an excellent example of the 'charm offensive' strategy so well used in the world of public relations these days. Far from dwelling on the scenes of urban deprivation so beloved of the doom and gloom merchants, this hi-tech and zappy video concentrates on the sunny uplands which can be reached by dint of hard work, humility and effort. In an age in which we sadly have to acknowledge that visions of the next world have somewhat lost their attraction for the young, due in no little part to the abdication of many teachers from their responsibilities for religious education, it is up to the positive thinkers in our ranks to supply visions of what can be attained in this world. To those who consider that these visions are already displayed at frequent intervals during the commercial breaks on television, we can only reply that not enough use is made of these well crafted productions by teachers who have a misguided sense of suspicion of the worlds of commerce and industry.

My Struggle
Author: Fred 'Tiger' Thompson
Published by Nonesuch Press, London

This is an autobiographical account by the much publicised headteacher of an East London school. In it he recounts the innovative managerial methods he used to combat a blighted situation of falling rolls, dilapidated and vandalised school buildings and local gang warfare amongst the youth of the community.

This volume, dictated to his deputy whilst they both awaited trial, will be of particular interest to those who see outdoor pursuits as the key to character building. The faint-hearted may have been dissuaded from purchasing the book by some of the more irresponsible reporting by the yellow-bellied and trendy-lefty (sic) tabloid press of the recent court case, in which the author and his methods were the subject of a hopelessly one-sided critical scrutiny following the unfortunate fatalities. The weaker-kneed brethren may take some comfort from the fact that approaches to keel-hauling are only lightly touched upon in Chapter 12. It is a mere footnote to the main theme of the benefits of discipline, obedience and humility, which resulted from the programme of compulsory community activity for which the school has become rightly celebrated.

A touch of verisimilitude is added by the first-hand accounts from the photocopied logs of some of the earliest participants in the 'survival weeks'. It is quite uplifting to see the developmental spiritual growth which appears to be in inverse correlation to the strength of the handwriting. The fact that hardened ruffians of this kind were impelled to write prayers begging for forgiveness, to a deity they had in the past reviled, demonstrates, to my own satisfaction at least, that Thompson's managerial grill may have a much wider application than is generally thought to be the case by some of the more squeamish of the mollycoddlers whose weepings and wailings were so rightly dismissed by Justice Jenkins in his landmark judgement in the High Court last week.

The author is now writing a sequel, to include a personal account of his incarceration and the subsequent court proceedings, entitled: 'Them as dies'll be the lucky ones.'

(Note to reviews editor: never again accept a reviewer recommended by the author's cronies, no matter what methods of persuasion they employ.)

Educational Management Across the European Union
Edited by Elfriede Hafenstaengel
Published by Proletarian Press, Nice

This so-called book is a series of badly prepared, poorly translated and hastily printed papers given at the 6th annual conference of educational management in the EU, held at Nice in the Summer of 1996. This heavily over-subscribed conference followed those at Monte Carlo, Baden Baden, Estoril, Windsor and Mallorca. Many of those prominent at the previous conferences managed to find time in their busy schedules to 'keep the flame of European educational management burning', as Professor Hafenstaengel so poetically expresses it in her mercifully brief foreword.

This foreword is presumably the professor's excuse for claiming an editorial function, as there is precious little evidence elsewhere in the volume that anyone has taken an ounce of care in cobbling together these travesties of academic papers. A real editor might just have spotted, for example, that the paper by Jean-Pierre Lanson deftly translated as: 'Educational Management: Whither Europe?' bore an uncanny resemblance to the contribution by the same author entitled: 'European Educational Management: *Quo Vadis?*' in the conference proceedings published after the Windsor jamboree.

There are, admittedly, some more original contributions in this latest collection, notably the somewhat emotional plea for a multicultural approach advocated in 'Northern Ireland's Message for Educational Management in Europe: A Modest Proposal' by Máirtín S.O'Conchúir. It is certainly an interesting perspective on multiculturalism to advocate the complete segregation of the Protestant and Catholic populations of the whole island.

The author seems to be of the view that the almost universal educational segregation in Ulster to date has only been accompanied by bloody sectarian violence over the last quarter of a century or so because of its very lack of absolute totality. Never one to shrink from a logical conclusion, he argues that harmonious and peaceful multicultural co-existence will only ensue once the Protestant enclave is physically, as well as mentally, walled off from the rest of the island. The notably impartial writer of this paper does admit, however, that there might be a sad tendency for the Protestant heretics not to see that this would only be for their own protection, but he does not see this as an insuperable obstacle to the lasting progress which only his solution can bring about.

He condemns all the other peace initiatives in the province, in typically measured terms, as 'the contemptible ramblings of demented idiots.' Somewhat surprisingly, I am given to understand that some of his colleagues, from the province but of a different religious persuasion, produced a counter-blast at the conference which was strongly deplored by their mainland colleagues as 'not in the true European tradition of harmonious collegiality'. It is, therefore, not included in the conference proceedings.

A Businessman Looks at Education: managerial words of wisdom for the groves of academe

Author: Dean Banato
Published by McGuffin-Price, New York

It was one of the publishing trade's less happy strokes of timing this year that this book's publication date was only a week before Banato's sudden departure for Paraguay. The FBI's current investigation into the $6,000,000 deficit in his holding company's accounts should not, however, prejudice the reader against Banato, who is stoutly proclaiming his complete innocence of any charges

that might be levelled against him. He continues to maintain his story that the emergency flight was arranged at very short notice after his doctor's warning of the need for a rapid change of climate on health grounds.

It is, after all, always a salutary experience for those of us in education to have our organisational practices scrutinized by an outside observer from the more hard-nosed world of commercial management. Indeed, rarely a week passes without some jumped-up dope peddler casting his or her beady eye on the incredibly antediluvian antics that pass for management in the world of education. Banato's approach might strike some of the staider pedagogues as somewhat iconoclastic, but there can be no doubt that his proposed solutions to, for example, the alleged problems of over-staffing in the world of education, in the chapter entitled 'Downsizing Downstream', are refreshingly straightforward.

The real joy of the book to this somewhat jaded reviewer's eye is the vivid use of language. Phrases such as 'giving her a concrete handshake' leap out of the text and grab you by the throat, if not the jugular vein. There may be those pedants who will try to cast doubt on the feasibility of importing into education in the UK some of the rather more unsentimental practices of Chicago business, but even these quibblers should see the acute relevance, for those of us familiar with the problems of computer viruses, of the concept of 'carrying cholera to the competitors'.

Banato's healthy contempt for inspectors of all kinds could also be an attribute that some of our more fearful headteachers might care to cultivate. That Banato was able to obtain so many favourable reports on his business practices over so many years from 'independent' observers only goes to bear out his precepts about the old ways of winning over the potential opposition still being the best.

Sayonara Kaizen, or Beyond Toyotaism
Author: James Just-in-Time Johnson
Published by Teamwork Publications, Newcastle upon Tyne

This is an account of how one headteacher incorporated Japanese work practices into his school and thereby transformed its culture. Indeed, so enthusiastic is Mr. Johnson about Japanese managerial methods that he claims to have taken them to new peaks of perfection undreamed of by the founding fathers of Kaizen and Total Quality Management.

The fanatical dedication of his staff to the meticulous execution of their very clearly specified tasks apparently has to be seen to be believed. Johnson argues that this stems from the fact that staff encourage each other to suggest ways, through their nightly Quality Circles, in which their tasks could be carried out in ever more improved ways. There are photographs in the book showing staff with stop watches timing each other on their way to and from the staff room. 'There is a happy game-playing spirit in the school that motivates all the staff to work at a faster than normal pace,' claims Johnson.

The loyalty of staff to their 'quality work teams' is such, according to Johnson, that the former hierarchy of managerial posts is no longer required. 'Quality improvement leaders' are appointed by Johnson only for the duration of a particular project (although he prefers to talk in terms of 'natural leaders emerging as the need arises'). At the end of each project, some leaders have their mandate renewed for the next project whilst others do not. This fluid and flexible structure helps to keep all the staff on their toes, according to Johnson. 'No longer do I have to contend with heads of department acting like feudal robber barons,' he says. 'There'll be no signing of mini-Magna Cartas in this school. All we need here are the individual two-line contracts which all the staff sign, to the effect that they will carry out efficiently and effectively any duties the head deems reasonable. As I never make unreasonable demands, there's no problem.'

The mutual self-surveillance procedures amongst the staff have also made considerable savings for the school staffing budget. Johnson is fond of referring to his 'Senior Management Team of One' which he describes as 'lean and mean', and he is proud of the fact that, apart from his own undisclosed salary, the piece work rates on which all members of staff are paid are uniform throughout the school. To avoid the competitive back-biting and envy associated with the usual hierarchical pay systems, Johnson 'harmonised' his piece work rates on those previously paid only to his manual workers. 'There are no class distinctions amongst the workers in this school,' he proclaims proudly.

Johnson's main claim is that he has gone beyond the managerial practices of 'Toyotaism', perhaps best known in the UK through their use in the Japanese motor car 'transplant' firms. Sadly, however, we will now never be able to debate this with Johnson himself at the nationwide series of seminars on the subject which he was due to lead in the new year. The unfortunate and mysterious incident which has made this book a posthumous publication is still the subject of police enquiries.

The Psychoneural Cognitive Transformation Plan
Author: V. Z. Dimitriov
Published by Gloucester House Publications, London.

Every once in a long while a book appears which revolutionises our thinking about the educational process. Unfortunately, this is not that book. It may have been readable in the original Bulgarian edition, but I doubt it. My suspicion is that it lost something in the original, never mind the translation. The version as we now have it looks less like a translation into English than a translation into psychobabble. Perhaps it is a translation from Bulgarian psychobabble into English psychobabble? In general, one word is never used when five or six could be used instead, and I guess there was some prize going at the time for sentence length combined with the number of polysyllabic words (as you can see, this becomes addictive after a while).

Stunningly banal statements of the obvious are supported by references to a string of apparently learned but highly obscure publications. Not only do I doubt whether any reader will ever be tempted to follow up these references, I have grave suspicions that, in many cases, Dimitriov himself never went beyond finding the title for citation. In other cases, he went so far as to find some trite sentences which are trotted out as 'quotations'. They rarely add anything but increased boredom to the reader's appreciation of the original statement of the obvious. This form of medical disorder is known in the trade as 'acadanaemia' and so far it has invariably proved fatal for all those who succumb to it. There is growing worldwide evidence that the disorder results from a viral infection, so we could soon be faced with a pandemic in the world of academe.

Much of the psychobabble in the book which is not just a complex restatement of the obvious is outrageously perverse, not to say bizarre. This 'highly original' element purports to be based upon research studies conducted in Bulgarian schools. This probably means that the writer occasionally popped into his local primary school for a cup of coffee on his way back to his flat in Sofia.

It is books like this that give politicians a good name. They provide justification for statements such as the following by Fred Neanderthal (Back to Basics Party): 'I have an excellent rule of thumb when evaluating academic books on education. If they come up with findings that accord with my prejudices, there is no point in my reading them in the first place. If they come up with findings I would not have expected, they are clearly badly researched and therefore not worth considering.'

The ultimate mystery surrounding this apology for a book,

which is really a monument to a misspent academic life, is how the author could stay awake while writing it. This is not a book to put down easily. Indeed, to paraphrase Dorothy Parker, much effort will have to be expended to hurl it as far away as possible. The weight of the tome would make it the ideal practice implement for a shot putter.

Alternatively, if you fancy a good long read in your slippered feet by the warmth of the antique fireside on a cold Winter's evening, then this book should provide sufficient heating material – if you can find the right sort of kindling to get it alight in the first place.

The New Government Initiative On Teacher Supply
Author: I. Sycophant
Published by Crawler Press, Westminster

With the raising of the pupil-teacher ratio in our schools to 100 to 1, it has become abundantly clear that the nation faces a crisis of teacher over-supply in the years ahead. The government cannot be blamed for this, although there are a few on the loony left who have tried to whinge along those lines. Suggestions that the economic problems of recent years have had anything to do with this eminently sensible readjustment of the average class size are a gross calumny. It is true that the government's number one spending priority has had to be the defence of the realm in recent years, but who would sleep safe in their beds unless they knew that our coasts were secure against the potential threat raised by a resurgence of nationalism amongst the natives of New Caledonia?

Nevertheless, it is obvious that this latest reform was inspired not by the thought of possible economies of scale, but by the independent findings of the 'Righthinking Policy Research Institute' funded by the Ling Tee Po Foundation. This research has pointed to the dangers of over-protection, to which the young of our once glorious nation have been exposed by the excessive numbers of teachers in the education system.

It seems obvious, once it has been pointed out, that the lack of independence and self-reliance now so prevalent amongst the young is a direct result of the mollycoddling they have received in schools notorious for their fostering of dependency relationships. The government measures to ensure obligatory part-time employment of the state educated young from the age of eight may have run into occasional little local difficulties at the implementation stage, it is true, but the reports of a few unfortunate accidents have been sensationalised beyond all decent proportion in left-wing media circles. In time, a grateful nation will come to see the wisdom of the young pioneer battalions.

This advance will now be complemented by the teachers' volunteer units, where redundant pedagogues will find they still have a service to render to the state.

Secret lives
(In tribute to
James Thurber on the
centenary of his birth)

'THE SHARE PRICE is going into free fall.' The accountant's voice, thin and reedy at the best of times, was now taking on the shrill, high-pitched tone of a man fast approaching the end of his tether. 'Our competitors are hovering like vultures, just waiting for the final death throes before they come in for the pickings.'

'Our shareholders are selling out in droves, just like rats leaving the sinking ship' echoed Ms Drover, fast losing her usual composure amidst the general desperate panic. 'If it goes on like this, we'll be calling in the receivers in the morning.'

Bill Jenkins carefully brushed away an imaginary speck of dirt from his immaculate Armani suit, and there was not a blink of his icy, steel-blue eyes behind the gold-rimmed spectacles as he gazed at the panic-stricken board of which he was the chief executive. Under his unflinching stare, their hysteria gradually subsided as they realised the old man was going to make one of his measured pronouncements.

'I strongly advise you to take the opportunity to boost your own personal shareholdings in the firm by every means possible before the market closes tonight,' he said in the languid drawl that had become his trademark. 'If you have to put up your own grandmothers' lives as collateral, don't hesitate for a moment,' he continued, as an ironic smile played around his thin lips. The board was transfixed by his words like a bunch of rabbits confronted by a stoat.

What did BJ have up his sleeve this time? The old man had pulled their chestnuts out of the fire too many times before for them to doubt his wisdom now. The 'merger' two years ago, which had sounded the death-knell of their major rival at the time, was only the last of a set of astoundingly audacious coups that had, over the years, earned BJ the sobriquet of the Dawn Raider. He must know something that escaped them all for the moment. All they knew was that something big was in the air, but whether it was another takeover, or a further massive guarantee from the Bank of Shanghai or whatever, was something that for the moment was BJ's secret.

'I propose a vote of full confidence in our chief executive,' piped the accountant.

'Carried unanimously, I see,' said BJ. 'Anyone for a game of squash this evening?'

★ ★ ★

'Well?' said the chair of the governing body. 'So just what *do* you propose to do about the falling rolls, headmaster?'

Bill Jenkins was startled out of his reverie by this typically blunt question from his typically blunt chairman, Tom Johnson. It was quickly followed by a reminder from the chair that since the previous catchment area agreement had lapsed, aggressive campaigns by their neighbouring schools were eating into their annual pupil intakes. The negotiations with the Bank of Shanghai were going to have to be postponed for the moment.

'I was wondering if we couldn't put another advertisement in the local paper,' Bill muttered in response, his faltering words sounding feeble and lame even to himself.

'We've tried that before,' countered Tom, strongly implying that it hadn't worked then and he was damned if he could see why it should work now.

'I think my deputy with responsibility for marketing has some suggestions, Chairman,' said Bill, desperately hoping that one of

Anthony Blenkinsop's dreary and lengthy sermons on the applicability of commercial techniques to the public sector would stall them long enough for him to collect his thoughts.

★ ★ ★

'How did you get them to agree to your proposal, Godfather?' queried his acting *consigliori* in incredulous tones. 'Don Tomasino and his family were dead against the idea when we met at Rizzio's last week.'

'Now they're just dead,' responded BJ in that hoarse whisper which had resulted from receiving too many blows across the windpipe from the rubber blackjacks of his youth.

'But what about the opposition of the Sollozo faction?' continued the *consigliori*, still failing to comprehend how the seeming disaster of the previous week's meeting could have been transformed into the apparent triumph of the moment.

'I made them an offer they couldn't refuse,' whispered the Godfather. 'Nobody is going to muscle into my territory and start hustling me. When the day comes that I can't protect our turf, I'll hand over to Tony and start to grow roses.'

The *consigliori* winced at the thought of dull Tony in charge of the family and then grinned inwardly to himself as he realised that the Godfather saw that as such a far-fetched proposition as to make the very idea of his retirement an hilarious joke. Now there would be sharp boundaries around their recruitment territory again and an end to the in-fighting between the five families that had threatened to blow their town sky high. He felt good to be living under the protection of the Godfather, and wondered yet again at the steely resolve and ruthless determination that lay well hidden behind the apparently mild exterior. Many had underestimated the Godfather and they had all paid a very high price for their poor judgement. The *consigliori* shivered a little at the thought of the various ugly ways in which that price had been exacted, crossed himself and went about the Godfather's business.

★ ★ ★

As he turned the key in the ignition, the sudden realisation that his car might be booby-trapped snapped Bill Jenkins out of his daydream. No, here he was again in the school parking lot. Sicily and the USA suddenly seemed worlds away. The meeting of the governing body was over, and he was still smarting at the way he had been treated by the chair. It wasn't his fault, he thought, if the people on the estate in the middle of which his school was situated had apparently decided that procreation was no longer in fashion. As he drove past the boarded-up windows of some of the more derelict of the local properties, he wondered to himself why any parents from further afield would ever dream of sending their progeny to his school. The rain lashed against the windscreen of his Vauxhall Astra and, even with the wipers working overtime, it was not easy to make out his route along the dimly lit roads of the estate.

★ ★ ★

He was only too well aware that they were losing altitude fast. The round of tracer bullets which had killed his tail gunner had also damaged the rudder in some way, so that the plane was now limping its way back from Berlin like a wounded eagle. Squadron Leader Jenkins had always known this lone bomber raid on the Nazi capital was a potential suicide mission. A lesser man would not have volunteered to try to give the Hun a bloody nose so early in the war, when everything was stacked in favour of the Germans.

'We know you're the only man for this job, BJ,' Churchill had said to him when explaining the mission. 'We've got to divert enemy attention from our airfields and provoke the swine into going for our cities instead. Otherwise the Battle of Britain is lost.' Well, they had certainly succeeded in punching a few holes in the jolly old Reichstag. Now all he had to do was to bring the broken-backed bird home and get his surviving crew safely into hospital. He felt their gaze as they lay bloody but uncomplaining on the floor of the bomber. They knew the old man had never failed them yet, and he was damned if he was going to start letting them down now.

Through the mist and fog, he could just about make out the Belgian coast. That must be Ostend, he thought – soon be home to Blighty now. He was almost down to sea level now, and the spray from the waves was hitting the cockpit and making visibility even worse. If only his right arm would stop throbbing with pain.

★ ★ ★

It was at the very last moment that he realised the traffic light was at red at the crossroads near his home. He jammed on the brakes, to come to a halt precisely on the white line. That would have been some touchdown, coming in on a wing and a prayer he thought.

But before he could drift off again into another daydream, the lights were at green again and he was fast approaching his own front door. His wife was waiting up for him as usual and she poured him a stiff whisky and ginger, which she had long recognised was an absolute necessity for him after a meeting of the governing body. She felt obliged to ask him how it had gone, but she knew what the answer would be and dreaded hearing the same old story yet again. As he began to drone on interminably about the meddling fools who thought they could tell a professional like him how to run his own school, her mind wandered.

★ ★ ★

'Just the usual run in with Jerry,' BJ was saying. 'Took a bit of flak over Berlin, but nothing to make a song and dance about. I wouldn't mind you taking a look at this arm, though, old girl. Perhaps you ought to get out the needle and thread this time. Be as good as new when you've given it the once-over. I can't see it stopping us stepping out on the town tomorrow night and tripping a bit of the light fantastic. You'd better buy yourself a new creation from the milliner's, by the way. I understand we're going to be invited to Buck House because of this trip. Something about another gong.'

Bill Jenkins wasn't the only member of the household who found fantasy land a happier place in which to dwell.

A dying breed

1 May 2010

I am beginning this statement because I suspect I will not stay long in my present post, and I feel it is important to record for posterity what might well be the last will and testament of a progressive liberal headteacher while we are still only a very endangered species in the UK. When we are extinct, as I fear could soon be the case, there may be some far distant generations who may be interested to know what made us tick.

I ask myself how it has all come to this very sorry pass. I suppose the most obvious contributory factor has been the almost unbroken Conservative Party domination of national politics for a period of what is now over thirty years. For most of that time, the majority of the citizenry of this country has been unable to envisage any other possibility. Only in 1997, with the Lib/Lab coalition election victory, did it look briefly as if this hegemony might be broken. The stock market crash that year and the subsequent collapse of the coalition produced instead the second election of that year and the almost inevitable Tory victory under the leadership of Sir Michael Portcullis. But this is perhaps just the greatest of the many 'might have beens' over this long period.

It was only post-1997 that the greatest blows against me and my kind were struck. The end of local government in the UK in 1998 took away a lot more than the old LEAs, but as far as education is concerned, that was the greatest shock. Suddenly finding all our schools privatised, we had to adjust to the voucher system with almost no lead-in time to make adjustments. The trauma was intensified by most of my headteacher colleagues finding themselves placed on short-term contracts by the new régime. Having more than 50% of our annual salary on performance pay almost exclusively related to our schools' positions in the league table results for each year was perhaps the unkindest cut of all.

There were loud protests of course, particularly from those heads in the areas of greatest social deprivation. These were more muted, however, after the withering sarcasm of the Secretary of State for Education, Sir Peter Lilliput, at the North of England Education Conference in January 1999. Those of my colleagues running schools in what Lilliput referred to as the 'Old Third Division North' were told in no uncertain terms that if we displayed any talent we would soon be snapped up by those schools in the premier league. Otherwise, it was down through the Vauxhall Conference League on the way to oblivion.

It wasn't just the heads who could go down-market either. Schools which had once had fine reputations in their area found that they were only as good as their last year's results. The fall in pupil rolls following relegation was generally catastrophic for the finances of the schools involved. To have to sell half your staff in a buyers' market was heart-breaking for any head with an ounce of compassion.

Of course, those heads with any compassion left by this stage soon found what a handicap this quality of mercy was to them. I well remember the sleepless nights I suffered after being forced to tell all the over-45s on the staff that I couldn't afford to keep them on the payroll any more. It gave me no pleasure at all to see grown men and women, many of whom had been star teachers in their time (and some of whom still were), weeping openly in the staff room. Few of them found suitable employment elsewhere. I'm almost glad now that so many have shuffled off this mortal coil in

the intervening years, because at least the flow of begging letters has considerably diminished.

Later generations of teachers seem attuned to the futility of such behaviour, and they appear to accept that they can only be employed as supply teachers with no possibility of a permanence of contract. The apprenticeship model they follow now that the teacher training institutions in higher education have been abolished has certainly meant that their lowly position in society is borne in upon them from the earliest stages of their days as pupil teachers.

The irony is that the politicians of that era now seem like models of moderation compared to those that followed. It was not long before a new generation of 'free marketeers' elbowed aside the old guard they had accused of going soft in their old age.

My own strategy for survival in the midst of all this mayhem was a variant of that 'internal emigration' adopted by the citizens of Central and Eastern Europe under the former Communist regimes. If they could preserve their basic value systems under the watchful eyes of the KGB, the Stasi and the rest of the police systems, then I was sure I would be able to maintain my liberal progressive ideals until the darkest days had passed.

'Keeping the torch of learning alight during the Dark Ages' was the way we used to refer to it when we had our monthly secret meetings. 'We' in this case meant the headteachers of the progressive faith who used our own homes in rotation as meeting places for discussions where even the officially proscribed subjects such as sociology could be given a decent airing, as opposed to the bureaucratic indecent burial at the crossroads at midnight.

In the earlier period, the voucher system worked reasonably well for those heads like myself whose schools were in the leafy suburbs and who had years of good relations with the local middle class community upon which to draw. As long as you kept your head down, you could avoid the cluster bombs which seemed to be falling ever more heavily on my less well favoured headteacher colleagues. I should, of course, have heeded the words of Pastor Martin Niemöller, who also only realised as his own fate was sealed that, by not speaking out when the Nazis came for the categories of victim to which he did not belong (Communists, Jews etc.), he was only preparing for the evil day when the Nazis turned up on his doorstep and when there was no-one left to speak out for him.

After all, I, and others like me, had witnessed the destruction of Her Majesty's Inspectorate in the early stages of all this. If the Crown was no protection, it was hardly surprising if teacher preparation in higher education was practically defenceless when the final onslaught came. The teaching unions were in no position to offer useful support at any level in education after the emasculating laws against unions in general.

In my own case, it was not any single decision that brought about my downfall. The process was cumulative. First of all, I did not put up defences to prevent children with behavioural problems from joining the school. Then I failed to exclude them at the drop of a hat when those problems manifested themselves in the classroom. This meant that when 'exclusion fever' had reached its height, we were receiving an undue proportion of 'problem cases' rejected by other schools. It was bad enough for recruitment that the school acquired in the locality the nickname of the 'sin bin', but this was compounded when the travellers' site was constructed in the near vicinity and I accepted their children into the school.

Most middle class parents who withdrew their children from the school after that offered implausible rationalisations for their decisions, and a few had the good grace to look guilty about it, but there was the odd parent who was frank enough to say that his or her offspring were not going to be brought up with 'the gypos' kids'.

I know that the newer breed of 'entrepreneurial' heads thought I was mad to go down this road, and a few of my competitors were not above intimating to prospective clients that I was, at best, a trifle eccentric, but I couldn't turn my back on children in need. Unfortunately, of course, such 'weakness' on my part soon meant that our position in the league tables began to fall. This only happened slowly to begin with over a period of years, but in these last few years the process of 'decline' has speeded up as the rate of withdrawals has increased. This has inevitably put me at loggerheads with a growing proportion of the staff, who understandably have seen their own jobs threatened by these developments. Lately I have had the feeling that remarks I have made to staff in confidence about governmental policy in a number of areas have no longer found the support that once they had. It would not surprise me even if some of the newer element were to denounce me to the authorities.

As I write this, I am becoming conscious of the fact that two men in grey raincoats are approaching the house. I am sure this is all part of my incipient paranoia, but perhaps I'd better put these notes in the safe place before I go to answer the door . . .

Editor's note: May 10th, 2040

The 'safe place' was indeed secure, and it is thanks to this that we have unearthed these notes some three decades later. Perhaps we can reasonably conclude that the newspaper reports at the time of the breakdown and subsequent 'death from natural causes' of this headteacher are at least now open to more than one interpretation.

Death of an educationalist

F ROM TIME TO time those of us on the editorial board entrusted with the sacred duty of keeping this magazine, *Managing Schools Today,* on the road meet to discuss whether we need new regular features. The Algonquin Round Table it ain't. Those of you familiar with the wit and wisdom of Dorothy Parker and her circle will recognise that we would have a hard time matching the care and sensitivity of that group. It was after all one of that select coterie who went to visit Dorothy in hospital after her second or third suicide attempt. On observing her bandaged wrists he came out with the immortal line: 'Tut tut Dorothy. If you carry on like this you'll make yourself sick!'

We lesser mortals content ourselves with pointing to the more hilarious misprints of the last few editions and making other such ribtickling sallies. Most of my suggestions for spicing up the magazine are cut down in their prime by the legal eagles who can spot a potential for libel almost before the idea has left the ground. This is what has sparked off my latest venture, because you can't libel the dead. Hence the obvious niche for an obituary column for those who have died after a life-time of mis-management in the wonderful world of education. Just to give you a flavour of the treats you might have in store I have written a totally fictitious obituary. If this should whet your appetite for more, please write to the editor, and then I can by-pass the nit-picking committee that keeps turning down my suggestions for agony aunts and the like. Just to avoid another spell in the hulks, may I again underline the fact that the obituary which follows bears no relation to anyone still alive in high educational places or, for that matter, dead in any other place. If anyone should be so unfortunate as to actually bear the fictitious name below I now extend my commiserations, but I must stress that I have never met you, read about you or even, as far as I am aware, heard your name mentioned in passing.

OBITUARY FOR SIR BRIAN T. WITHERSPOON-FLICK 1936 – 1993

Brian Flick, as he was known in his early days, suffered a number of vicissitudes in his upbringing which may have left deep scars which he nevertheless bravely attempted to hide throughout his life from those of us who were privileged to work with him. He was orphaned at a relatively early age after the tragic car accident in which his mother and father and other siblings perished. It was one of the constant sorrows of his life that the police were never able to bring to justice whomsoever it was who had tampered with the car brakes. After that he passed fairly rapidly through the homes of a succession of aunts and uncles who never seemed able to adjust to his creative but demanding nature. Even at this early age he was never one to suffer fools gladly, although his definition of a fool was a little more wide-ranging than that which most of us would have adopted. His teenage years in the orphanage are still something of a mystery because he was always reluctant to discuss this period of his life, and all the orphanage records were destroyed in the conflagration of 1957 in which the warden and his wife also perished.

By this time, Brian was at university, and it was just before arrival there that he added the Witherspoon to the Flick by deed poll. Indeed none of his contemporaries at university, as far as we can ascertain, were aware that he had not only taken the hyphenated surname between the orphanage and the university but had also added the letter of a non-existent middle name at the same time. All this was in keeping with his existentialist philosophy. Tomorrow was always the first day of the rest of Brian's life. He had no time for those who maintained that there was a fixed core of human identity. Indeed he liked to talk about the many lives of Brian, often asserting that he could see no resemblance to his current self in the few photos which existed from his childhood and youth.

His activities as an undergraduate at Easttown University were so many and varied that it was little surprise when he only acquired a third class honours degree in Politics and Economics. He always maintained that his real education took place in the 'university of life'. Certainly, the stagecraft he acquired in the Drama Society, and the many friends and acquaintances he developed through the university rifle shooting club were to prove invaluable to him in the years ahead. Much of the small legacy which he acquired from his parents when he reached the age of 21 was generously spent throwing parties for his fellow students. It must have been at this time that he first recognised his legendary prowess at holding his liquor and staying sober when all around him were becoming garrulous in their cups. Immediately after taking his degree he spent a year in Palermo broadening his cultural perspectives and acquiring his life-long passion for all things Sicilian. He then moved universities to take his postgraduate certificate in education, thus qualifying to be a teacher and at the same time obtaining exemption from National Service. It was one of the major regrets of his life that he was never able to follow up on the field of battle his captaincy of the rifle club and his well-deserved blue in that sport.

In the following four years he taught in six schools. There were those, both at the time and later, who argued that this was an excessive rate of change, but he was always a 'driven' man, and from his work during those four years he was able to claim truthfully throughout his subsequent career that he had teaching experience at all levels from primary school to FE college. He then took up a post at St. Bartholomew's College of Education as it then was. During his three years there he obtained not only a Master's Degree in Educational Psychology, but also a wife. In these politically correct times it would probably be regarded as less than acceptable that she became pregnant by him while still working as his special study student. Nevertheless it has to be recorded that she obtained a first-class degree and a bouncing baby boy shortly after each other. It was at this time that he made the decision to have a another geographical move and took up the post of lecturer in education at the University of Sludgeville. His poor first degree in a subject field not then taught in schools might have been construed as an obstacle to his obtaining such posts in education, but the Dean of the Faculty of Education at that time was the father of one of his old university classmates and fellow party goers. He took Brian under his wing immediately and his contemporaries were quick to spot the very special relationship which existed between the two men despite their age difference. Indeed the then Dean tolerated a degree of familiarity from his protégé which he would not have accepted from others.

It was at this time that Brian began to publish those seminal papers on the hereditary factors in dyslexia which were to culminate in the award of his PhD and form the basis of his subsequent academic career. The strikingly similar results which emerged from the 'identical twin studies', not only from his own research but from those studies conducted by his research assistants, provided conclusive evidence for his main hypothesis. It is true that in recent years there have been mutterings in the groves of academe about these studies, but this seems to have been little more than idle and envious gossip based on the fact that nobody has been able to trace the more recent whereabouts of Ms Brightside and Ms Townley who were his research assistants at the time. Those in the university who have claimed never to have seen these research assistants even when these studies were being published are simply displaying their ignorance. I can well recall a string of young female research workers who seemed to be constantly dancing attendance on Brian at that period in his career. It is the in the very nature of university research that such young women rarely find tenure and very soon turn to the joys of domesticity where their maiden names are quickly forgotten.

As a direct result of this pioneering academic research, Brian was appointed to the chair of education at Westview University, becoming the youngest Professor in the land in the process.

Admittedly he did not stay there long but that had less to do with his alleged reluctance to actually teach classes (his colleagues were more than willing to take over his teaching duties so that he could bring more prestige to their faculty by his further research publications), than with his unfortunate domestic circumstances during that period. By this time the proud father of three children, the sudden departure of his wife and family was to prove a heavy cross for him to bear. It was not surprising in the circumstances that he sought other female company to make him forget that which he had lost. The divorce proceedings may indeed have been 'messy', but it was surely wrong of the Vice-Chancellor to set so much credence on the testimony of Brian's first wife who was clearly hell bent on character assassination so that she could obtain custody of the children and guarantee a substantial alimony settlement. Some of the sexual peccadilloes to which she referred at the divorce hearings could only have been the products of her own overheated imagination. Much of this was unnecessary as I recall Brian telling me at the time that he had absolutely no intention of tearing the children away from their mother and he had, indeed, little contact with them thereafter. This was the kind of selfless remark which gives the lie to all those who have accused him of ruthless egocentricity.

It was no doubt a relief to all concerned when he became a member of Her Majesty's Inspectorate and left Westview. The anonymity in which HMI reports are shrouded makes it difficult to know which bear his particular imprint. It does seem most unlikely, however, that he played a major role, as now alleged by some of his colleagues, in writing the reports which extolled the virtues of mixed-ability teaching, large comprehensive schools and child-centred education which appeared in the 1960s. It has to be admitted that this does not seem to fit easily with the fact that when he left HMI and opened a private consultancy service in the 1970s, his name figured prominently amongst those denouncing the excesses of 'progressive education' in a string of grey papers which brought him to the attention of Central Office. His second marriage to the only daughter of the Party Chairman was truly an affair of the heart.

His rise to become the Vice-Chancellor of his old alma mater,